WOMEN AND FOOD SECURITY
ROLE OF PANCHAYATS

About the Editor

Pradeep Chaturvedi, is a well known development expert involved in Food Security process for the last 20 years, since FAO's World Food Day was established in 1981. His expertise lies in project planning, implementation and management with emphasis on technology transfer and skill building. A number of pioneering projects and studies of national and international significance have been conducted under his guidance. At present, Mr. Chaturvedi is also working as a Consultant to FAO's Regional Wood Energy Development Programme for Asia.

He contributed significantly in the preparatory meetings of FAO's International Conference on Nutrition, in 1992; and FAO's World Food Summit, in 1996. He concentrated on motivating NGOs in India and the Asia Pacific region; and reflecting their viewpoints at the Global Summits.

Mr. Chaturvedi is a Graduate in Engineering. He is a Fellow of The Institution of Engineers (India) and the recipient of FAO's World Food Day Silver Medal 1991.

Mr. Chaturvedi has authored 6 books and edited 24 books related to sustainable development, food security and energy management, and has addressed a number of national and international conferences.

WOMEN AND FOOD SECURITY
ROLE OF PANCHAYATS

Edited by

PRADEEP CHATURVEDI

CONCEPT PUBLISHING COMPANY, NEW DELHI - 110059

ISBN 81-7022-873-5

First Published 2002

Published and Printed by
Ashok Kumar Mittal
Concept Publishing Company
A/15-16, Commercial Block, Mohan Garden,
New Delhi-110059 (India)

Phones: 5648039, 5649024
Fax: 091–(11)–5648053
E-mail: publishing@conceptpub.com

MESSAGE

This eighteenth observance of World Food Day marks the fifty-third anniversary of the founding of the Food and Agriculture Organisation of the United Nations (FAO) in Quebec City, Canada.

This year's World Food Day and TeleFood theme is "Women Feed the World". This theme was selected to pay tribute to the significant role of women in agriculture, fisheries and forestry and their enormous contribution to household and national food security.

In many countries, particularly in developing countries and in agrarian societies, the production of staple food, cash crop and livestock rely heavily on women's labour. Most of their backbreaking work is unpaid or grossly underpaid and little attention is paid by agricultural tool producers, researchers, and extension workers to alleviate women's drudgery. Rural women play a key role in ensuring household food security, especially in times of crises. Their strategies for coping during droughts and famines, namely by cultivating secondary food crops in small plots around the house and keeping small livestock, are testimonials of the resilience and ingenuity of women in the face of crisis. Women are involved in harvesting, processing and marketing of food products, and possess a vast knowledge of local biodiversity, which they apply in ingenious sustainable production systems on their small plots. They are universally responsible for food preparation for their families. In this capacity, they are often the first to suffer from environmental degradation, as they have to travel farther and farther from their homes to gather the requisite fuelwood and water to feed their families.

Notwithstanding their invaluable contribution to household and national food security, very limited attention is dedicated to the vast potential that women farmers and agro-entrepreneurs represent in terms of achieving optimal agricultural productivity and reducing post-harvest losses. This is one of the reasons why, on this World Food Day, we still face the morally untenable situation that more than 800 million men, women and children in the world suffer from chronic hunger and malnutrition. At the World Food Summit convened by FAO in 1996, leaders from 186 countries pledged to reduce the number of hungry people in the world at least by half by 2015. They also acknowledged "the fundamental contribution to food security by women, particularly in rural areas of developing countries, and the need to ensure equality between women and men". To this end, the Plan of Action adopted by the Summit specifically calls for the promotion of women's full and equal participation in the economy, and for the introduction and enforcement of gender-sensitive legislation providing women with secure and equal access to and control over productive resources including credit, land and water.

World Food Day observances provide an opportunity to review progress made at country level in the follow-up to the Summit and is an occasion for mobilizing the various sectors of civil society in the campaign to achieve the objective of Food for All. Clearly achieving the Summit goal and winning the war against hunger and malnutrition at country level require the contribution of many actors – national and local governments, NGOs, the private sector, youth, the media, parliamentarians, the academic and scientific communities – and last but not least, both men and women farmers.

In the framework of World Food Day, I launched in October 1997 "TeleFood", a televised appeal for global solidarity and support as part of the follow-up to the Summit. This year's edition of TeleFood will be held from 16 to 18 October. During these three days, TV programmes and broadcasts of related events will span the globe with images and information, highlighting women's contributions to the fight against poverty and hunger and urging solidarity to ensure food security for all. Last year, TeleFood was watched by over 500 million people who learned about the scourge of hunger and malnutrition and responded by contributing more than US$ 2 million to help poor male and female farmers to produce more food, improve nutrition and family incomes to lead lives free from hunger. Currently, 159 TeleFood small-scale projects provide tools, seeds or other essential supplies for food security activities in developing countries.

This year's World Food Day/TeleFood theme should also help create the enabling political, social and economic environment required for the eradication of hunger and poverty. By drawing attention, on the one hand, to the significant contribution that women make against many odds to food production and food security, the Organization also wishes to enhance the understanding and responsiveness of policy and decision makers to the needs and priorities of women engaged in agriculture.

By implementing the commitments made at the World Food Summit, including those calling for equality between women and men in terms of access to productive resources, the battle for food security can be won. I hope this year's World Food Day/TeleFood will serve as a milestone for the advancement of all the women who help "feed this world".

JACQUES DIOUF
Director General
Food & Agriculture Organisation
of the United Nations.

Message on the occasion of World Food Day/Telefood 1998
– 16th October, 1998.

PREFACE

Addressing Food Security issues through the Panchayati Raj system has been an issue of interest to all of us as it envisages development planning close to the communities where needs assessment and subsequent programme can go hand in hand. The United Nations Organisations in India have been working together on this issue through the Inter-Agency Working Group on Food Security and Nutrition, exploring the current situation and its opportunities for strengthening food security mechanism. On several occasions the issue has been discussed with experts in this field and those closely involved with the communities. It is widely understood that women as food growers and processors, home and community managers, and as planners of development play an important role in achieving Food Security and should be recognized as such individually as well as through their groups and elected Panchayat members.

World Food Day celebrated on 16th October, 1998 focused on the theme "Women Feed the World". Significance of role of women in agriculture is realized in India. Recently women's empowerment through Panchayati Raj has also offered them an opportunity to decide at the village and local level and ensure food security. This movement being new requires a few models to be developed.

I am glad the Government of Maharashtra took the lead and prepared a Project Proposal for developing a Model on Food Security and Panchayati Raj.

It is encouraging to note Government of Maharashtra's interest in exploring the possibility of strengthening their Panchayati Raj System in ensuring Food Security at the community and household level with special focus on participation of women's groups. Exchange of views and ideas, experiences from the field and expert insights at the consultation on 16th October, 1998 guide the Government of Maharashtra in concretising the concept for establishment of a small pilot programme and assist us in the United Nations to support such activities in Maharashtra and elsewhere in India.

PETER ROSENEGGER
FAO Representative in India and Bhutan

INTRODUCTION

The 73rd Constitution Amendment established third tier of governance through the Panchayati Raj Institutions at the district, block and village levels. This empowerment enabled the people to decide on a number of activities and implement them as considered appropriate. The empowerment as a result of the Constitutional Amendment does not automatically pass all the benefits to the rural people. There are a number of steps that have to be planned and implemented to ensure that the people really get the power in their hands. A study on the Status of Panchayati Raj Institutions indicated a direct positive movement towards empowering Panchayats. At the same time the allocation of business has made it amply clear that Panchayats will have greater role in programmes related to poverty alleviation and food security.

FAO's basic concern has been on food and nutrition security for the common man. However, issues relating to poverty are found to have a direct bearing on food security on a sustainable and self-supporting basis. Empowerment to purchase food is a major concern which can only be achieved through poverty alleviation and income generation programmes. Public Distribution System has played a significant role in preventing masses from serious food shortages.

Realising significance of the Panchayati Raj Institutions in India, the FAO and the Indian Association for the Advancement of Science have been focusing on issues that link panchayats with food security. A number of discussions and consultations were organised in the past that helped to crystallise the idea and also to develop a strategy that will help and support a larger programme on food security in India. Integration of panchayat model of governance with food production facilities at the panchayat level need certain models to be developed for their application. In this regard the Department of Rural Development of the Government of Maharashtra made a sincere effort in developing a model for the backward and malnourished areas of Maharashtra. The idea for developing a model was acceptable, in principle, to the Government of India in the Ministry of Rural Areas and Employment. This acceptability motivated us to organise a national consultation was considered appropriate for the national consultation before finalising the concept into a project proposal for developing a model.

The World Food Day, 1998 was chosen as an occasion to organise the national consultation with the theme "Panchayati Raj and Food Security : Opportunities for Women's Participation".

The consultation was inaugurated by Dr. N.C. Saxena, Secretary in the Ministry of Rural Areas and Employment and the Round Table was chaired by Dr. M.S. Swaminathan, President, Dr. M.S. Swaminathan Foundation. The Round Table discussed the concept of the model for implementation in Maharashtra, as presented by Mr. Ramesh Kumar, Secretary, Department of Rural Development, Government of Maharashtra. The Round Table provided some important inputs.

A number of distinguished authors related to agriculture and food provided their inputs in the form of written text which were circulated to the participants for discussion.

Various papers presented at this Round Table and discussions have been compiled and are being presented alongwith other contributions from distinguished authors.

Also four documents have been added as Annexures to give an idea about FAO's approach on Food Security in 1982 i.e. when World Food Day programme was launched; at the time of World Summit on Social Development and the World Food Summit.

We hope this volume will be of interest to the readers.

PRADEEP CHATURVEDI

New Delhi
September 15, 2000.

CONTENTS

LIST OF CONTRIBUTORS

M.S. Swaminathan
President, M.S. Swaminathan Foundation.

Pradeep Chaturvedi
Secretary General, Indian Association for the Advancement of Science.

N.C. Saxena
Secretary, Ministry of Rural Areas and Employment.

George Methew
Director, Institute of Social Science.

Sudha Pillai
Jt. Secretary, Ministry of Rural Areas and Employment.

Suresh K. Sinha
Former Director, Indian Agricultural Research Institute, New Delhi-110012.

Arbind Ghose

Devinder Sharma
Agricultural Development Expert.

Sushma Sharma
Reader, Lady Irwin College, Sikandra Road, New Delhi-110001.

Kalyan Bagchi
Director, Nutrition Syndicate, New Delhi.

Seema Puri
Senior Lecturer in Food and Nutrition Institute of Home Economics, Delhi University, Delhi.

Subhadra Seshadri
Head, Department of Food and Nutrition, Hon. Co-ordinator, WHO Collaborating Centre for Nutrition Research, MS University of Baroda, Baroda.

Shashi Prabha Gupta
Technical Adviser, Department of Women & Child Development (Food and Nutrition Bureau).

K.P.A. Menon
President, Indian Association for the Advancement of Science.

P.V. Rao
Executive Director, Manipal Industrial Trust, Manipal.

C. Gopalan
President, Nutrition Foundation of India.

Ramesh Kumar
Secretary, Department of Rural Development, Government of Maharashtra.

1

WOMEN IN AGRICULTURE, ENVIRONMENT AND RURAL PRODUCTION IN INDIA

FOOD AND AGRICULTURE ORGANISATION

GENERAL PROFILE

Population

India's estimated population in mid-1996 was 954 million. Rural population accounted for 71 per cent (1991 census). India is a country of extreme diversities in language, religion, caste and socio-economic class. Hindus account for 83 per cent of the population and Muslims 11 per cent (EIU, 1997). There are also other religions – Christians, Sikhs, Zoroastrians, Buddhists, Jains and Jews (ESCAP, 1997). The population growth rate is little under 2 per cent. Population density is 273 per sq. km. The total fertility rate in 1992 was 4 per cent. Women constitute 48.1 per cent of the population (EIU, 1997). In 1992-93 only 9.2 per cent of the households were female-headed. (ESCAP, 1997).

The sex ratio in India is 93 women to 100 men. This situation of a strongly male-biased sex ratio is attributable to infanticide or neglect of girl children. This ratio is 9.4 in rural areas compared to 8.9 in urban areas. The excess of men in urban population is really attributable to higher male migration to urban areas (ESCAP, 1995).

Education

The adult illiteracy rate in India was 48 per cent in 1995. Women had 62 per cent illiteracy, whereas men had 34 per cent (UNDP, 1997). Both male and female literacy rates are substantially lower in rural areas than in urban areas.. This rural-urban difference is more pronounced in the case of women. Among the rural female population in the age group of 7 years and over, the literacy rate is 30.4 per cent, whereas it is 63.9 per cent among the urban female population. Moreover, the difference between male and female literacy rates is much higher in rural areas compared to urban areas (ESCAP, 1997). Both gender and residential differentials in the literacy rate vary considerably across the states.

Labour

The Indian work force participation rate is 37.7 per cent (1991 census). The rate for women is 22.7 per cent, which is less than half the rate of 51.6 per cent for men. The pattern of women's participation in the labour force varies across the country depending upon geographic region, caste, socio-economic class and formal and informal sectors. The rural female participation rate is 27.2 per cent, nearly thrice as much as the urban female participation rate of 9.7 per cent. The percentage of labourers employed as main workers is higher among men than among women. In the case of marginal workers, this proportion is larger among women than among men. The majority of the main workers (66.8 per cent) are employed in agricultural and allied industrial sectors. The proportion of women employed in this sector is 80.7 per cent, compared to 62.7 per cent for men. In rural areas 89.5 per cent of the total female employed are engaged in the agricultural and allied industrial sector. In urban areas manufacturing, processing, servicing and repair, when it is in the household, absorbs larger proportions of the total female employment compared to men. The reverse is true when it is other than household work. Industries which employ more women than men are Bidi and match manufacturing, cotton textiles, cotton spinning, cashewnut processing, tobacco stemming and redrying, canning, preserving and fish processing (CSO, 1995).

The Human Development Index (HDI) rank of India in 1997 was 188th out of 146 countries, indicating low life expectancy at birth, low educational attainment and low income. This demonstrates difficult developmental challenges confronting India in human resource development. The Genera-Related Index (GDI) rank of India in the same year was 118th out of 146 countries. This illustrates the human development gap was further aggravated by substantial gender disparities.

AGRICULTURE

In India around 70 per cent of the population earn their livelihood from agriculture (EIU, 1997). The Indian agricultural production area is delineated to 15 regions based on water resources, irrigation pattern, rainfall distribution, soil characteristics and cropping pattern. Characteristics and potentials of agriculture strongly vary across the regions. Each region has distinct characteristics and potentials for agricultural production (Meena, 1991).

Rural Indian women are extensively involved in agricultural activities. However, the nature and extent of their involvement differs with the variations in agro-production systems. The mode of female participation in agricultural production varies with the land-owning status of farm households. Their roles range from managers to landless labourers. In overall farm production, women's average contribution is estimated at 55 per cent to 66 per cent of the total labour with percentages much higher in certain regions (Venkateswaran, 1992). In the Indian Himalayas a pair of bullocks works 1064 hours, a man 1212 hours and a woman 3485 hours in a year on a one-hectare farm, a figure which illustrates women's significant contribution to agricultural production (Singh in Shiva, 1988).

Women provide one half of the labour in rice cultivation in India (Stanford, 1986). In the plantation sector women are the crucial labourers (Shivaram, 1988). Depending on the region and crops, women's contributions vary but they provide pivotal labour from planting to harvesting and post-harvest operations.

Traditionally, women had usufruct rights to the community land. But after the land reforms, land titles were given to men, denying women's access to land. In general, women in tribal households enjoy more decision-making power than women in many other Indian households because of their greater contribution to household income (Yadama, Pragada and Pragada, 1997).

Crop Production

India has a variety of crops grown in irrigated and rainfed areas. Rice, wheat, jowar, maize and bajra are the major foodgrains. Oilseed, sugarcane, cotton and jute are the important cash crops. Likewise, tea and coffee are important plantation crops. India's agricultural production systems also include a wide range of horticultural crops.

Rice is widely grown in Southern, Eastern and Northeastern states. Wheat is mainly grown in Punjab and Haryana. Jowar and Bajra are important foodgrains in dryland areas. Assam and West Bengal are famous for tea, whereas Karnataka, Tamil Nadu and Kerala are coffee and coconut producing states.

In the highly diversified Indian context, no simple gender division of labour exists with regard to crop production. In certain areas in India women play a key role as seed selectors and in seedling production. Their knowledge on seeds and seed storage contribute to the viability of the agricultural diversity and production. As weeders, women contribute to crop management. Women prepare and apply green and farmyard manure. As integrated pest management practices are introduced, it could be expected that women's work will increase due to more labour-intensive activities.

An example of gender involvement in crop production in Kolli hills in Tamil Nadu is presented below.

Livestock

In India, livestock plays a multi-faceted role in providing draught power for the farm, manure for crops, energy for cooking and food for household consumption as well as the market. In animal husbandry women have a multiple role. With regional difference, women take care of animal production. Their activities vary widely ranging from care of animal sheds to processing milk and livestock products. In livestock management, indoor jobs like milking, feeding, cleaning, etc. are done by women in 90 per cent of families while management of male animals and fodder production are effected by men (Narayanan, 1997).

Women accounted for 93 per cent of total employment in dairy production (World Bank, 1991). Depending upon the economic status, women perform the tasks of collecting fodder, collecting and processing dung. Dung composting and carrying to the fields is undertaken by women. Women also prepare cooking fuel by mixing dung with twigs and crop residues. Though women play a significant role in livestock management and production, women's control over livestock and its products is negligible. The vast majority of the dairy cooperative membership is assumed by men, leaving only 14 per cent to women (MOA, 1991).

Forestry

The Indian population, particularly the rural, is highly dependent upon forests. Fuelwood contributes 84 per cent of the total household energy consumption (UNDP, 1997). There are 66.5 million tribals in India and with few exception, the majority of them are forest dwellers (FAO, 1997). Unfortunately, forests are deteriorating massively due to encroachment of agricultural production, mining, construction of dams, industrial and railway demand. The country has been losing 1.5 million hectares of forest cover annually (GOI, 1998). In India about 16 per cent of the total geographical area is covered by woodland and forests (EIU, 1991).

Gender roles in using forest resources vary widely depending upon the region as well as socio-economic class and tribal affiliation. Rural Indian women's interface with the forests is varying – gathering, wage employment, production in farm forestry and management of afforested areas in the community plantation (Saxena, 1991). In India, women are the major gatherers and users of a much more diverse range of forest products than men. Depending upon the socio-cultural variations among different communities, primarily Non-Timber Forest Products (NTFP) are collected by women and timber by men (Sarin, 1998). In several parts of India, large proportions of the population depend on NTFP as their main source of livelihood. Apart from fodder and fuel, women collect food, medicinal plants, building materials, material for household items and farm implements. Sal and Tendu leaves are primarily collected by women. As women are the ones who have traditionally been collecting forest products, they possess the knowledge of properties and potential uses of these products.

Fisheries

India is among the top ten fish producing countries in the world contributing about 3 per cent to the world marine fish catch. About 5 million people in the coastal areas carry out fishing and allied activities for their livelihood (Devraj *et. al.*,1997).

In India, nature and extent of women's participation in fishery varies across the states. Fish drying/curing, marketing, and hand-braiding and net-mending are the main areas of women's involvement in Tamil Nadu, Andhra Pradesh and Orissa. Women are also involved in shrimp processing in these States. In addition, in Andhra Pradesh, women are engaged in mollusc and shell collection on a seasonal basis in a few places along the coastline. However, marine fish capture is a men's domain (FAO, 1998). Among the mangroves of Bhitarkanika on the Orissa coast, both women and men fish in the fresh waterestuarine areas. Men cast nets while women and children catch fish with hands. But fishing by boat in the flood tides is exclusively performed by men (Kanvinde, 1997). In contrast, women's participation in small-scale fisheries is very limited in West Bengal. Even ancillary industry, which in the other Indian east coast states is a women's domain, is dominated by men, as a relatively low number of days in a year is spent on actual fishing. In the fishing villages, fish drying/curing is performed by both women or men who do not belong to the fishing community. In coastal aquaculture, women are involved in prawn and seed collection to a very limited extent (FAO,1980).

ENVIRONMENT

Sharp decline in common/real estate property land on one hand and the deterioration of the remaining land have jointly contributed to hardship for the rural community, particularly for women of the poor households. Deforestation has increased time and distance involved in grazing and collection of fuel and food. Distance to forests or other sources of fuel, type of farming system, etc. have explained increases ranging from 435 minutes to 5 hours in women's work time (World Bank, 1991). Moreover, it has also threatened income generating opportunities for women by affecting livestock rearing and collection of NTFP. Reduced or non-availability of NTFP has shifted women from self-employment to wage employment. In areas where traditionally men also collected fuelwood, deforestation resulted in decrease in men's participation, as it was no longer possible to collect fuelwood in build (CPSW, 1992).

Women play a key role in both land use and management. They supply inputs from the forests as fertilizer to the soil as well as fodder for the cattle, which produce fertilizer for the soil. In India there are women-headed movements for forest protection such as Chipko and Appiko.

Women have also been the source of knowledge relating to conserving and maintaining the quality of water. Depleting water resources have also impacted women severely in terms of longer walk and more work, as they are a principal collectors of water. Nonetheless women in different states have varying degree of involvement in water collection.

In Mizoram in the north-eastern hills women have the knowledge of animal ecology ; that male hunters acquire (Krishna, 1997). In the island ecosystem of Lakshadweep, off the coast of Kerala in the Arabian sea, women are more conversant with the resources around their homes and along the reef and shore, while men who go further afield to fish and collect coconuts are more knowledgeable about land, lagoon and sea (Hoon, 1997).

RURAL PRODUCTION

Women in rural India generate income in various ways. Women are highly involved in processing of the NTFP, particularly in small-scale enterprises. This includes basket, broom, rope making, tasar silk cocoon rearing, lac cultivation, oil extraction, and bamboo works, etc. Women constitute 51 per cent of the total employed in forest-based small scale enterprises. However, this does not mean that men do not have any role in these activities. Among the scheduled caste weavers in Orissa, men collect grass for basket making while women cure it and make the basket (Kanvinde, 1997). In the Jeypore Tract (Orissa), men and women are equally involved in collection, processing and marketing of forest products such as grass, bamboo and resin (Sharma, Tripathy and Gurung, 1997). But among some tribals in Arunachal Pradesh, all the tasks related to basket-making is considered men's work (Krishan, 1997).

FOOD SECURITY

In India, food security as a national objective was placed on the policy agenda much earlier than in other developed and developing countries.With the Green Revolution technology, India has achieved self-sufficiency in foodgrains. However, India had a share of 40 per cent of all those people in the world that were regarded by the World Bank as being below the poverty line in 1990. Data for 1993-94 suggest 19 per cent of the total population are below the poverty line (EIU, 1997). In India, rural poverty was 39 per cent whereas urban poverty was 30 per cent in 1994 (UNDP, 1997). Approximately 35 per cent of the households below the poverty line are headed by women (Venkateswaran, 1992). Women have a share of only 25.7 per cent in earned income. The proportion of pregnant women (aged 15–49) with anemia is as high as 88 per cent (UNDP, 1997).

Women's key role in the production of major grains and minor millets illustrates their invaluable contribution to the food security. In addition, women play a crucial role in ensuring supply of food as food vendors and post-harvest processors of livestock and fishery products. As major buyers of family food and meal-makers, women ensure adequate food security. As primary providers of nutrition to the young children, women are the major decision makers in ensuring nutrition to the next generation.

POLICY AND PLANNING FOCUS

- Given the diversity of the agro ecological system and the resulting wide varieties of farming systems, it is important that state level efforts in gender planning are supported by gender/sex-segregated data pertinent to local situation.

- The current efforts on creating agricultural data and gender information in farming systems across the country should be coordinated and the available informations should feed into the planning process.
- Planning at the local Panchayat level should be gender-sensitive and should have gender/sex-segregated information to support for local development efforts.
- Agricultural education institutions and training centers should develop regular curricula to integrate a gender approach in all technical areas of agricultural sector.
- Existing policies related to targeting women and gender-equity should be widely communicated to all involved development work including women clientele.
- Review of the land right policies and implementation of land distribution for gender equity and women's land rights.
- Farmer's right initiatives should explicitly address concerns of women farmers.

PROGRAMME FOCUS

- Develop programmes to train Panchayat leaders in gender-integrative participatory approaches and local planning.
- Develop programmes for rural women to build leadership skills for managing agriculture community-based development activities.
- Develop economic and political literacy programmes for rural women to utilize development inputs effectively.
- Support agriculture extension in-service training programmes and other relevant agricultural curricular activities to support gender-sensitive extension agents.
- Put in place appropriate institutional mechanism for information exchange and cooperation between the agencies that focus on women's affair and agriculture-related technical activities.
- Support women-managed rural production and marketing

ventures in horticulture, floriculture and post-harvest processing in commodities.

- Provide technology training and input support to women to take advantage of emerging high-value agribusiness sector including bio-technology and forest products.

KEY FACTS

- Indian Population is 48.1 per cent women and 51.9 per cent men.
- Female illiteracy is 62 per cent whereas the male illiteracy rate is 34 per cent.
- The labour force participation rate of women is 22.7 per cent, less than half of the men's rate of 51.6 per cent.
- In rural India, agriculture and allied industrial sectors employ as much as 89.5 per cent of the total female labour.
- Women have extensive work loads with dual responsibility for farm and household production.
- Women's work is getting harder and more time-consuming due to ecological degradation and changing agricultural technologies and practices.
- Women have an active role and extensive involvement in livestock production, forest resource use and fishery processing.
- Women contribute considerably to household income through farm and non-farm activities as well as through work as landless agricultural labourers.
- Women's work as family labour is underestimated.
- There are high degrees of inter-state and intra-state variations in gender roles in agriculture, environment and rural production.

2

HUNGER FREE AREA PROGRAMME : A Step Towards Food Security

M.S. SWAMINATHAN

The concept of Food Security and Women in relation to the Panchayats has to be viewed very carefully. We should look at food security at the level of the individual, as we say the household is not a homogeneous unit. All studies have shown that women as mothers, and also many times as girl children are under-nourished relatively within a family. One should speak of nutrition security for an individual so that it is in respect of gender of members of the family.

There are three components to food security, one is availability in the market – that today is not a problem in our country. That is related to production. Today India has surplus food, largely because over 200 million are undernourished. But, availability is there. Second is the economic access, which is limited to income generation.

This has now become our principle problem and has not received enough attention. Basic issue is: "How to create non-farm employment"? The worst sufferers are those who have no assets – the landless poor. This is the main problem. Usually, the maximum they can get is minimum wage or in Maharashtra the employment generation scheme, EGS is below the minimum wage. It has been purposely kept that way.

The third element that has not found place in this particular presentation in absorption of food. I said, availability, absorption, and access. The biological absorption and retention of food depends on safe drinking water and environmental hygiene. In fact, in our studies show that even when a family is able to digest a lot of food, there is doubt of infection. So if we really want to have food security at the level of protective and healthy life, one must look at availability of food access to it and finally ability to digest it.

We have looked into the concept of food security at the level of individual and converting that into practical programme. We call it hunger free area programme; and fortunately, the National Agenda of Governance, NAG, of BJP and its allies promises hunger free area programme which aims at removing hunger in five years. Whether the government's National Agenda programme is converted into real action plan, but Chairman's comments nevertheless it is a good thing. It is a starting point. Awareness is a starting point for analysis of action.

There are seven elements, which the Panchayati Raj Institutions can take up, helped by civil society organisations and the government departments. The first is to leave it to the people to identify who are hungry. When we did not do that we usually found that only 10-12% were identified. In 7 districts of Tamil Nadu, this has been done under a government sponsored programme. Mr. Karunanidhi was kind enough atleast to set the ball rolling. Tamil Nadu was also a pioneer in universal nutrition. Noon meal programme by former Chief Minister, Mr. M.G. Ramachandran has proved to be a boon to millions of children. The first step was to identify those who are hungry. We find three criteria: first is no education; secondly no jobs and thirdly no house. Using these three parameters you find that the total number of people below poverty line is 30-40 per cent, and the problem looks staggering. If you break it up at the level of Panchayats then the problem is much more manageable.

Prof. Amartya Sen's famous concept of entitlement of people. What we did was, we made household entitlement cards? I have got one in Tamil Nadu, for one Panchayat referring to 145 anti-poverty scheme. Now, they have got 145 anti-poverty schemes. People do not know about these schemes at all. Information empowerment is very important. Only 10 per cent of those, who are entitled to avail of the scheme really benefit and, therefore, you do not provide full money for it I think this is very important. Today you have computerised, network. You can create all access systems. In Delhi women, with education up to 8th standard are also operating the Computer. They are highly skilled, provided the method of training is good; and therefore, we have a modern technology of information.

The third is protein calorie malnutrition which is very widespread; and that is why it has been mentioned in the Maharashtra Report very clearly, various kinds, whatever mechanism you have including the targeted public distribution system. System was also one answer to this question, of reaching those who were so far unreached. There are very many mechanisms. Dr. K.P.A. Menon and I were in the government, in 1979, Rural Godown Scheme and Trysem schemes were introduced. Now the same is called the grain bank. That was how it was conceived. The fourth area of hidden hunger is very important. The World Food Summit has quoted, if 800 million children, women and men, go partially hungry tonight, 2 billion suffer from iron deficiency alone.

In fact we are starting a programme in the Dharmapuri district of Tamilnadu with FAO's help on the total elimination of micro nutrient deficiencies. Largely through the agriculture-horticulture pathway.

I would also suggest that the word coarse grains, should not be used as that is a British terminology. They are very nutritious grains. In fact, if you analyse nutritionally, they are very rich in iron, very rich in calcium. We have been fighting to change this terminology, because British called many of these grains as coarse grains in relation to good grains, i.e. wheat and rice. They also called pea as pigeon pea, because they were feeding to chick and pigeon. The coarse grains should be renamed atleast. You start this initiative calling them nutritious grains. Now this micro-nutrient deficiencies are very serious and that we must eliminate. The 5th area is biological absorption. Clean drinking water is a major problem. Number of surveys have shown that the greatest obstacle to food security at the level of the individual today is the biological absorption and retention. Environmental hygiene is a concern. Livelihood is the sixth concern. For economic access to food mention has been made of micro credit. I think there are number of opportunities. Trying to utilize credit intelligently, and particularly, if they are controlled by themselves, it certainly works well and the amount of credit makes a lot of difference. But, the credit has to be supported by services. The micro credit and services should be linked to creating jobs and providing employment. Nobody talks about employment in this country, even when they are adding 17 million children every year, to the population. According to the Planning Commission, 100 million new livelihood are to be created in next 7 years, Prime Minister mentioned it from the ramparts of the Red Fort on August 15. But, having said this figure, what is your strategy. It can be tackled only at Panchayat level. The 7th concern or programme is for pregnant women and children. A number of reports indicate that every third child born in this country is under-weight, low birth weight children and it is serious menace. On one hand we say that the emerging millennium is the knowledge millennium and on the other information on such basic issues is also not transferred. There is overwhelming evidence that there is adverse relationship between pregnant women's malnutrition, nutritional anemia and low birth weight children and brain development. This is reversible later. In other words, you are condemning children at birth for no fault of theirs. How do you then compete in a world, which is going to be dominated by intellectual property rights and so on. No more gold and so on or property, only the intellect. Bill Gates, showed clearly that. If you want to have a nutritional programme on food security, then look into all these aspects. Who are the real hungry. Consider the on-going schemes – both governmental and non-governmental which have been taken to the people. If it really reaches them to the people who are entitled to them the problem will be solved.

I hope that the Panchayati Raj Institutions will play an important role in ensuring food security.

3

LAND RIGHTS TO WOMEN : Will Ensure Food Security

N.C. SAXENA

The three themes, in relation to Food Security and Panchayati Raj are: Food Security, Panchayati Raj, and Women. Farming is no longer a household activity and nor can be developed only by government support. Role of the private sector is equally important. The Capital intensity in agriculture in India should be proportionate to the urban population. USA with 98 per cent urbanisation is expected to make capital intensity at 98 per cent. The capital intensity in India, making it proportionate to urban population, should make agriculture capital intensive to only upto 30 per cent. The capital intensity of agriculture should be reduced and the labour intensity should be intensified. In times to come, the unit for food security should not be household but the whole village as a composite unit and that is where the role of Panchayats become important.

Panchayats are searching for a role model. An ideal model of decision making will be the one which will diffuse in action and every member will be willing to take action and responsibility. Governments in a few States like, Madhya Pradesh, Kerala, Tamil Nadu and Andhra Pradesh have strengthened village Panchayats to get social development work executed through them.

Village panchayats then would be able to undertake a lot of development. It will also lead to satisfaction at the village level. Of course there is a possibility of social unrest. But, at the same time, there is again a sign of progress. If you want to change the political structure, if you want to change the structure of authority, there would always be resistance and that would often result in violence. Therefore, a bit of violence is a part of social change and that should be seen in that spirit. I think, the Panchayats have a lot of role to play in ensuring food security through management of natural resources.

It is basically land and water and in many places forests. If these can be integrated into planning for the activities of government departments perhaps through the Panchayats, then I think there will be lot of agricultural production and food production.

I always believe that women's participation would be meaningful only if authorities are interested; otherwise women may be feeding the world but would themselves go hungry unless they have land rights. I have often noticed this is a very controversial step. Unless agricultural land is recorded in the name of women farmers, they may be contributing their labour but they would not have control over the resources.

Women may also suffer from a number of handicaps. First of all, they do not have control over their own labour. Even when it is converted, they do not have specific power to use that capital the way they want. This can be sorted out only when women are recorded as land owners. In the Northern India, especially in Punjab, Haryana, Uttar Pradesh, Himachal Pradesh and in the State of Delhi, the law itself says that women cannot be land owners. When a land owner dies, the land would devolve only to male children and not to daughter. If there is no male then there is certain devolution. It is this law that is needed to be changed. There are other states that do not specifically deny the rights to women farmers of ownership, but again there are problems in recording. We have requested the state governments to examine their laws, because this hits basic fundamental rights in Articles 14 and 16 of the Constitution. Unfortunately, no one has challenged in the Court, this is the subject of political importance. In the last one year there has been a lot of debate in the newspapers, in Parliament about reservation of women. When it comes to giving rights to rural women on basic resources of land and water, nothing is mentioned. I had an opportunity to talk about this with the former Prime Minister, "Sir, you must say something about this in your speeches". He looked at me with great surprise and said, "Jats will never accept this". I think FAO can really help us, a great deal by supplying, or by focusing its attention on this particular issue as to which law and which particular section, or practice of the laws need to be changed. More work needs to be carried out in the field of studying the role of women in decision making, both at the level of users' committees as also in various laws which need to be changed, if we really want to give authority and empowerment to women.

4

STATUS OF PRIs AND FOOD SECURITY

PRADEEP CHATURVEDI

Introduction

The UN Inter Agency Working Group on Food Security and Nutrition decided to develop a joint UN Project on Panchayati Raj and Food Security. On May 12, 1997 a Study titled 'Present Status of PRIs in terms of their Role in Food Security' was assigned to the author to ascertain the status of Panchayati Raj Institutions, and to identify the thrust area of government activities to develop an outline for the prototype project. The study was completed by the end of June 1997. This chapter presents a summary of the same study.

Constitutional and Legal Aspects of Panchayati Raj Institutions

Panchayats have been the backbone of the socio-economic fabric at the village level in India. The new Panchayati Raj system was initiated after the Balwant Rai Mehta Committee Report in 1958. PRIs were established to enlist people's participation in rural reconstruction when the community development and national extension service (inaugurated in 1952). Following the report of the Committee on Panchayati Raj Institutions in 1978 (widely referred to as Ashok Mehta Committee Report) which argued for democratic local government focusing on party based elections, the State Governments of West Bengal, Karnataka and Andhra Pradesh attempted their own models of Panchayati Raj system. 74th Constitutional Amendment Bill was introduced on May 15, 1989. The new phase of Panchayati Raj Institutions initiated in the country after the Constitution 73rd Amendment Act, 1992 came into effect on April 24, 1993. The Articles of the Act made Panchayats responsible for following activities:

(i) preparation of plans for economic development and social justice.
(ii) implementation of schemes for economic development and social justice, as may be entrusted to them, including those in relation to the matters listed in the 11th Schedule.

The 11th Schedule of the Constitution had 29 activities for which PRIs were responsible.

The relationship amongst Union, States and PRIs is as defined in Article 40 of the Constitution in relation to Directive Principles of the State Policy. While the Federal Government has a right to sponsor schemes in national interest, *ad-hoc* announcement of projects by the Union and its direct entry into areas which directly belong to the local bodies, specially when it makes no commitment to continue their financing, not only reduce the PRIs to its sub-agencies or mere conduits for flow of funds, but also snatch the initiatives from them.

Among the 25 states, 7 states already had some kind of PRIs. Elections to all the tiers of Panchayats were completed in March, 1997, except for Bihar and the States which have been exempted under the Act; and the 6 hill districts of UP.

Appointment of Statutory bodies like the State Election Commission, State Finance Commission and District Planning Committee were also specifically provided under Constitution 73rd Amendment. All the states have appointed the Election Commission and the Finance Commission. Some of them had submitted their reports and the others were expected to submit shortly. Only 4 of the States, viz. Punjab, Rajasthan, West Bengal and Kerala accepted the same.

Present Status of PRIs in Selected States

Three important aspects involved in implementation of principle of constitutional obligations required for building institutions of self-government are defined as:

(i) Functional autonomy
(ii) Financial autonomy
(iii) Administrative autonomy.

Under *Functional autonomy,* the suggested list of all subjects of panchayats given in the 11th Schedule of the Constitution point towards functional domain to development activities only. The Panchayats have to be drawn into a wider spectrum of activities rather than development alone. Certain principles for the same could be as follows:

(i) The principle of efficiency
(ii) The principle of complementarity
(iii) The principle of clarity
(iv) Agency functions should not dominate
(v) Local level planning of local resources should be an important function of Panchayats.

Functional autonomy to be effective, needs strong backing of *financial autonomy.* Certain issues considered important for financial autonomy, largely arising out of the relevant provisions in the legislation can be identified as follows :

(i) The PRIs do not have independent taxing powers.
(ii) The tremendous potential of public contribution, both as a source of income and a means of promoting participation is demonstrated by some panchayats.
(iii) Important aspect of State Finance Commission.
(iv) Provision for independent budgeting by different tiers of Panchayats.
(v) Fiscal autonomy would be advanced if all authority regarding distribution of funds is vested in the district level authority.

Administrative Autonomy is yet another important aspect for the total autonomy of the PRIs. By autonomy is meant the freedom to select and supervise their personnel and administer their services as well as the degree of freedom within an enabling legal framework.

The report further refers to appraisal in 8 different States in regard to the Panchayati Raj programme implementation. These States include; Andhra Pradesh, Gujarat, Karnataka, Madhya Pradesh, Maharashtra, Rajasthan, Uttar Pradesh and West Bengal.

The *Finance Commission* of the Central Government which has submitted its report in 1995 has recommended an *ad-hoc* per capita grant of Rs.100 for rural population (based on 1971 census figures) for the period 1996-2000. This grant-in-aid works out to Rs.1095.23 crores per year.

Change in composition of PRIs with reference to tribal population was specially considered and the amendment was accepted in December, 1996. The latest Amendment will empower the tribals to take their own decisions and implement them in consonance with the customary law, social and religious practices and traditional management practices of community resources.

The study also pointed out to certain interventions that will empower women to undertake initiative to ensure household food security. This include the following :

(i) It is important to realise, for the sake of participatory rural appraisal, participatory planning and action by panchayats, that one set of key informants on food security are rural women. Panchayats should ensure to solicit their participation in order to learn about their knowledge gained through performing such activities.

(ii) Participatory sessions with women can identify women among the projects on self employment programmes on plantation of trees and plants so as to increase food availability and decrease their hardship and uncertainty in collection of food. The village women can suggest plants which they would like to grow.

(iii) Land reforms have so far avoided women's right to land. This anomaly has to be corrected, particularly in the context of female headed households. Food security for a third of the poors can be ensured by bringing these women into the ambit of land distribution. Land in their names is less likely to be sold.

(iv) Upgradation of traditional knowledge of farm women and

improvement in their traditional marketing skills will be the best agents of food security at panchayat level.

(v) It is important, in terms of food security, to identify what all the women would grow. Before the onset of the Green revolution, women usually had a patch of land on which they grew more nutritious food than the bulk cereal.

(vi) Women can effectively be involved in choosing and preserving the seed for the next sowing. They can be involved in developing seed banks for the local quality of grain that suits the dietary pattern of the people and are hardy to grow.

(vii) Women labour should be paid at par with the male labour. Removal of this discrimination under development projects can substantially improve the quality of life.

(viii) Cooperative grain banks have been installed in some of the villages. Women have been observed to be good managers of grain banks. Women should preferably be the managers of such grain banks established under panchayats.

(ix) Agricultural credit initiatives have indicated that women have excellent fiscal discipline. Timely and sufficient credit will be a great incentive to greater production. Promoting and supporting self-help groups, working as Rural Banks, is the best conduit for credit facility. Women managed Rural Banks can be promoted under women's management.

(x) Agricultural research at the moment is gender neutral which leads to marginalising women. Appropriate tools to suit the ergonomic of women farmers need to be developed.

Strategies for Attaining Food Security

The Government of India announced nutrition policy in 1993 and the National Plan of Action on Nutrition in April, 1995. Two major international conferences, the first namely, the International Conference on Nutrition was organised in Rome jointly by FAO and WHO in 1992. Second was the World Food Summit, again in Rome by FAO in 1996. FAO and IAAS organised an important intervention, National Symposium on Food Security for the Poor on October 4, 1995 and subsequently a National Workshop on

'Panchayats – The Key to Food Security' on July 15-16, 1996.

Report further defines that overall food security involves three basic issues of availability, stability and accessibility. The Constitution of India in Article 47 recognises the responsibility of raising the level of nutrition of the people among its primary duties. The minimum needs programme, started in the Fifth Five Year Plan, also included nutrition as an important component. Strategies for improving household food security include overall development strategies; accelerating growth in food and agriculture sector; stabilizing food supplies; increasing employment opportunities and improving access to land and other natural resources. The above mentioned strategies called for action under the following broad categories:

(i) Produce own food needed to attain food security.
(ii) Improve access to food through food trade, for which sufficient income must be generated.
(iii) Establish Public Distribution System to ensure regular supply of food.

The root cause for household food insecurity was identified as poverty and, therefore, actions related to poverty alleviation were important for ensuring food security for the poor.

The rural employment projects that have a bearing on food availability have been promoted by the Government through Jawahar Rozgar Yojana; Employment Assurance Scheme; Million Wells Scheme; Self-employment and Entrepreneurship Development Programme and Integrated Rural Development Programme.

PRIs have an important role in ensuring food security through food production, marketing, storage and distribution.

Public Distribution System that deals in six essential commodities, i.e. wheat, rice, sugar, imported edible oil, kerosene and soft coke, has a special role in insulating the consumer to a large extent from the impact of rising prices of these commodities and maintaining the minimum nutrition status of the population. Revamped PDS and the targeted PDS aimed at improving availability of essential commodities to consumers living in areas of relative economic disadvantage and different vulnerable groups under the poverty line have been identified as two major applications where PRIs have an important role.

UN Inter Agency Working Group on Food Security and Nutrition

The UN Inter Agency Working Group on Food Security and Nutrition was constituted in April 1996 under FAO's leadership with the immediate underlying goals of :

(i) follow-up to the World Declaration and the Plan of Action for Nutrition (International Conference on Nutrition in 1992) whereby focusing on the Indian National Plan of Action on Nutrition from 1995;

(ii) preparation for and follow up to the 1996 World Food Summit in Rome;

(iii) support to the formulation of the 9th National Five Year Development Plan; and

(iv) assist in implementation of other UN Conferences' recommendations in the context of food security and nutrition.

Programmes (relating to Food Security) of members of UN Inter Agency Group have been defined for the agencies like UNDP, UNESCO, UNICEF, WFP, FAO, THE WORLD BANK, IFAD, UNIFEM and UNFPA.

Training Institutions

To deal with the training requirements for the PRIs, the Ministry of Rural Areas and Employment has developed its training infrastructure. The National Institute of Rural Development, NIRD, is the main operating arm for the Government of India. 25 State Institutes of Rural Development (SIRDs) at the state level and 87 training centres are considered the main training arms for the government programmes. In addition, extensive support has been mobilised from a number of training and research institutions dealing with the issues relating to rural development. Whereas NIRD is comprehensively equipped with the facilities for conducting the training programmes most of SIRDs lack in proper training facilities.

Programmes of Selected NGOs

A review of an NGO, involved with the UNDP in food security matters was also conducted. ACTIONAID is an International organisation dedicated to help children, family and communities to overcome poverty and secure lasting improvement in quality of their lives. Actionaid has been working in India since 1972 and launched a Food Security programmes mainly in the State of Orissa.

Priority Areas of Activities for UN Assistance

The priority areas of activities that will be of interest to Government of India will be as follows:

(i) Capacity building through NIRD and its associated State Institutes;

(ii) Development of a Model of micro level planning and implementation for food security through PRIs and its testing in a few selected Panchayats in different parts of the country.

Conclusion

As a follow up of the report detailed discussions were held with the Ministry of Rural Areas and Employment, Government of India and the Department of Rural Development, Government of Maharashtra. Accordingly a concept outline has been developed by the Government of Maharashtra to initiate action in selected panchayats in Maharashtra.

5

PANCHAYATI RAJ AND FOOD SECURITY
Opportunities for Women's Participation

GEORGE MATHEW

After 73rd Constitutional Amendment became part of the Indian Constitution on 24 April, 1993 and the states were given one year to pass conformity acts, Article 243 B(1) says, "There shall be constituted in every State, Panchayats at the village, intermediate and district levels in accordance with the provisions of this part." Five years have passed. All States except Bihar, Jammu and Kashmir, Arunachal Pradesh and Union Territories of Pondicherry and Lakshadweep today have elected Panchayats. They are 'Institutions of self-government' according to the Constitution.

The new generation of Panchayats have seen more than 800,000 women getting elected to the Panchayats. When elections are completed in all the States and Union Territories, we will have about 500 District Panchayats, 6000 Block/Taluk Panchayats and 250,000 Village Panchayats. Women will be chairpersons in one-third of all these bodies. The positive aspect is that the base of Indian democracy has expanded considerably. It has brought to the fore large number of players who can contribute significantly in the process of governance and administration.

The critical question today is: how this development will help to improve the quality of life of the people. In this, of course, food security is an important aspect. Women's role and participation in ensuring food security is the issue before us. Will the new phase in India's democratic, decentralised governance bring in a qualitative change in women's role and participation in food security?

Schedule 11 of the Constitution has 29 subjects. According to Article 243 G(b), those schemes for economic development and social justice in relation to the matters listed in the Eleventh Schedule 'may be' entrusted to the Panchayats by the Legislature of a State. Among the 29 subjects, a large number are directly or indirectly related to food security. They are:

1. Agriculture, including agricultural extension;
2. Land improvement, implementation of land reforms, land consolidation and soil conservation;
3. Minor irrigation, water management and watershed development;
4. Animal Husbandry, dairying and poultry;
5. Fisheries;
6. Social forestry and farm forestry;
7. Minor forest produce;
8. Drinking water;
9. Fuel and fodder;
10. Poverty Alleviation Programmes.

It is important to remember here that although almost all the states in their conformity acts have mentioned transfer of these subjects, real transfer of subjects/schemes to the Panchayats have not taken place in the last 5 years or so. No rules, bye-laws are made. Some States feel that holding elections is the beginning and end of implementing the 73rd Constitutional Amendment.

The key to effective functioning of Panchayats is land reforms. And land reform is central to increased food production and thereby food security. Land reform brings about equity and fair distribution of resources in the rural areas. Unfortunately, the post-independent history of India speaks more of lip service for land reform than actual implementation. On the other hand wherever land reforms have taken place, today there are better working of Panchayats and better food security. The best case is that of West Bengal.

It is well known that in West Bengal the new Panchayati Raj phase (1978 onwards) was preceded by mass movements for changing the land ownership pattern (1976-77). The administrative action to ensure security of tenure of sharecroppers between 1977 and 1982 was a success mainly because of the involvement of Panchayats. By implementing the land reform the landed gentry's capacity to hijack the democratic system at the village level was taken out. Thus the uniqueness of the West Bengal Panchayat system is that it has brought into focus the issue of land reform in the creation of healthy Panchayati Raj. Therefore, it could be stated that land reform is inseparable from democratic decentralisation and the two are the "two legs" of the rural development programme. The Panchayat's credibility was established by the elected members' role in registration of bargadars, distribution of vested land etc. It may be added here that the task is not yet fully complete.

The interesting outcome of this two leg approach to rural development is that agricultural production in West Bengal has gone up. Nirmal Mukarji and D. Bandopadhyay in a critical study of Panchayats in West Bengal (1993) had stated that just going round the countryside makes it abundantly clear that there has been an upsurge of agricultural production in the State. Land reform has contributed to agricultural development because its direct beneficiaries, patta-holders and recorded bargadars were motivated to register high production. When the Mukarji-Bandopadhyay team visited Panchayats they were told that agriculture was on a rising curve. No doubt, Panchayats have played an important part in this encouraging development because they have been implementing agencies of both land reform and state interventions; they made local plans and set up priorities and goals. Panchayats also provided leadership to achieve these goals.

Till 1993, West Bengal did not have a sizeable number of women elected representatives. But when the opportunity came more than 35 per cent of the seats were won by women. However, through the political parties, women had participated in the election process and in the building up of movements before 1993 and that influenced the land reform and food production positively.

The Panchayats are the best instruments for bringing about changes in rural India. And now that women also can participate in these bodies in a big way, it is bound to change the relationships and power equations in the villages. Therefore, the vested interests are making all out attempts to defeat the goals set out for the new generation Panchayats. Not a day passes without stories of atrocities on women elected members.

Last year Gundiyabhai, Sarpanch of Pipra village in Tikamgarh district (Madhya Pradesh) hoisted the flag at the local school to mark the 50th year of Independence. She was of Chamar caste. The question was: how dare she touch the flag? On the way home after the programme, she was attacked. She became a victim of violence by upper caste men. Just, the other day we received a story from Orissa that a woman sarpanch who refused to part with JRY funds for Dussehra celebrations was stripped and robbed by her own Panchayat members. In Tamil Nadu, Leelavathy, the Madurai Municipal Councillor was hacked to death for bringing piped water to her constituency, thus causing serious loss to the contractors who supplied drinking water by tankers. These are some of the examples. What is amazing is that the women Panchayat members when convinced of the common good, they stand up to be counted, courageously act without caring for the consequences. Of course, in the process they pay a heavy price.

In this gloomy situation there are several success stories. Mrs. Fatima Bi, Sarpanch of Orvakal Mandal Panchayat of Kurnool district receiving the UNDP award this year for " Race Against Poverty" is one such achievement against several odds. She has brought not only food security but social security as well. There are several such stories. But as of now, failures are far more than success.

If women can come forward in a big way, they will succeed. Nearly 10 lakh women elected to the local bodies is a big force. Can the society benefit from their talents, abilities and capacity for leadership? Some of the problems to be tackled are:

1. Women's literacy, Education of the Girl Child – A policy shift for greater emphasis on the girl child and her elementary education.
2. Negative approach of those in power today – the political leadership at the Centre and State level, the officials and male members of Society – for women getting equal place in decision making bodies.

3. Gender discrimination – discrimination in wages, ownership rights.
4. With the heterogeneity that is India, prescribed common solutions are adding to the problems. Innovative and appropriate solutions for each context is lacking. There is no debate on social security.
5. Women have been at the receiving end all this time: whether it is natural calamities or man-made. Amartya Sen's concept of "missing women" as a result of discrimination in medical care, nutrition and general attention is a reminder in this regard. Can the new situation change it?
6. Many hurdles in the way of Panchayats becoming the Third tier of governance.

Even now the States have not found ways to bring a harmonious working relationship of line departments under the Panchayats – whether under Zilla Parishad, Panchayat Samiti or Gram Panchayat.

Elected women members to the Panchayats can contribute for ensuring food security – production, distribution and all other related aspects. But food security cannot be taken as a single isolated issue. It is part of the complex social and economic relations. With the large number of poor in the country, in every village, block or district food security should be on top of the agenda. The approach to solve the problem through administration, by the departments have failed. Now the only hope is democratically elected local bodies with increased participation of women. Women have shown that they could be successful in co-operatives, micro-credit enterprises and movements against social evils. The Panchayati Raj system is beckoning them to create history – a history of success in the sphere of food security.

Facts about PRIs in India - 3

Number of Elected Women Members
(As on May 31, 1998)

Sl. No.	States/UTs	GP			PS			ZP		
		Women	Total	%	Women	Total	%	Women	Total	%
1	2	3	4	5	6	7	8	9	10	11
1.	Andhra Pradesh	78000	230529	33.84	5420	14644	37.01	363	1093	33.21
2.	Arunach Pradesh*	–	–	–	–	–	–	–	–	–
3	Assam	7458	24860	30.00	745	2486	29.07	–	–	–
4	Bihar@	–	–	–	–	–	–	–	–	–
5	Goa	468	1281	36.53	–	–	–	–	–	–
6.	Gujarat	41180	123470	33.35	1274	3814	33.40	254	761	33.38
7.	Haryana	17928	54159	33.10	807	2418	33.37	101	303	33.33
8.	Himachal Pradesh	6013	18258	32.93	558	1661	33.59	84	252	33.33
9.	Jammu & Kashmir	–	–	–	–	–	–	–	–	–
10.	Karnataka	35305	80627	43.79	1343	3340	40.21	335	919	36.45
11.	Kerala	3883	10270	37.81	563	1547	36.39	104	300	34.67
12.	Madhya Pradesh	156181	474351	32.93	3169	9097	34.34	319	946	33.72

(Contd.)

1	2	3	4	5	6	7	8	9	10	11
13.	Maharashtra	100182	303545	33.00	1174	3524	33.31	587	1762	33.31
14.	Manipur	576	1556	37.02	–	–	–	22	61	36.07
15.	Orissa	28595	81077	35.27	1870	5260	35.55	294	854	34.43
16.	Punjab	23892	78983	30.25	326	2441	13.36	89	274	32.48
17.	Rajasthan	38791	119419	32.48	1740	5257	33.10	331	997	33.20
18.	Sikkim	27	1827	1.48	–	–	–	1	145	0.69
19.	Tamil Nadu	31548	94304	33.45	2295	6499	35.31	225	648	34.72
20.	Tripura	1809	5427	33.33	67	196	34.18	24	70	34.29
21.	Uttar Pradesh	174410	682670	25.25	14002	58165	24.07	648	2551	25.40
22.	West Bengal	22014	62172	35.41	3202	9516	33.65	227	664	34.19
23.	A & N Islands	229	667	34.33	25	–	–	10	30	33.33
24.	Chandigarh	22	109	20.18	2	6	33.33	3	10	30.00
25.	D&N Haveli	46	135	34.07	–	–	–	4	16	25.00
26.	Daman & Diu	25	63	39.68	–	–	–	5	15	33.33
27.	Lakshadweep@	–	–	–	–	–	–	–	–	–
28.	Pondicherry@	–	–	–	–	–	–	–	–	–
	Total	768582	2449759	31.37	38582	129871	20.71	4030	12671	31.80

Note: * Act has not received President's assent. @ Elections have not been held.

6

PANCHAYATS AND FOOD SECURITY

SUDHA PILLAI

First of all I would like to thank FAO and IAAS for giving me this fantastic opportunity to share the platform with no less an eminent person than Dr. M. S. Swaminathan. Sir, we have grown up reading about you. If we can hold up our heads it is because of the claim that we can rightfully make in our country that we have a large measure of Food Security at national level. When we come down to the micro level, as has been brought out very clearly, the situation is not so rosy. There are large segments of our society which are actually bereft of nutrition and the fruits of revolution. It is these people who cannot be reached through traditional approaches. I have the good fortune of dealing with the subject of Panchayati Raj. Liberalisation and decentralisation of governance are buzz words of *mantras* of the 90s, though both are poorly understood concepts. As has been brought out by other speakers, the 73rd Constitutional Amendment has given a constitutional status to Panchayats. Today the Gram Sabha is a Constitutional entity. So a revolution has been contemplated under the 73rd Amendment. However, when we look back five years after the law has been actually put in place, we find that our progress has been patchy. On the positive side, those of us who have made periodic visits to villages at different points of time find that there is a definite element of increased capacity and confidence. This notwithstanding some gruesome episodes that have been reported by Dr. George Mathew. It appears that there is a large majority of Panchayats, which are actually getting empowered. Even though by and large, departments of the State governments and Central government have not made Panchayats central to their schemes, it must be seen that at the local level State governments in most States have given many powers particularly to Gram Panchayats. There is a definite potential for a meaningful role in changing the lives of the poor and it is this that makes it possible for a Sarpanch to go to New York tomorrow and receive an award. Even States like Rajasthan, State government have given several rural development schemes, which are being implemented by Panchayats and this has resulted in positive changes among the elected representatives who are sincere – in women Sarpanchs, women Pradhans and also in members of Panchayats. Many elected representatives are able to take advantage of some of the efforts at capacity building. However, I would be not doing my duty if I did not point out what we have not done. Many States have not given powers in areas other than what we call Rural Development Department. There are several schemes formulated by the department of education, health and family welfare and women and child development and even agriculture which are meant for villages. We have recently studied 30 or 40 schemes of these departments and we find that at present Panchayats are not central to these schemes. Now this raises serious questions. This may not be deliberate. Many departments are not aware what they should do. They are very comfortable with the implementation of Centrally Sponsored Schemes by the State government departments. When we come to the State government we find that Kerala and West Bengal, Tripura and Madhya Pradesh, are proactive on Panchayats. In several other parts of the country, however, no serious efforts to devolve powers in respect of 29 subjects of XI Schedule. There are many departments which are very crucial in villages. This absence of devolution is partly because of threat perception that they will lose power and partly because there is a kind of difference about the capability of Panchayats to handle large sums of money. Recently what we have done is that we have talked to DFID, who are supporting a scheme called "Local Government Good Practice Scheme". We have asked governments to devise projects. Government of Kerala is expected to come up with a project for building up capacity of Gram Panchayats for two things – technical competence and competence in keeping accounts and in handling funds. Skills in this project can be transferred to other parts of India. This is important because the absence of such competence has become a reason for State governments to slow the devolution of powers.

There are also other struggles which are going on. There are several people in the State government who do not want to work with Panchayats. But taking stock of the entire situation, I would very confidently say that Panchayats are here to stay and each one of us has a contribution to make.

I am actually very thrilled and very encouraged to see that many people and agencies seek to foster Panchayats. FAO recognises that Panchayats can raise the level of food Security in vulnerable areas and among the vulnerable segments of our society. UNICEF are working with us to achieve what they perceive us their goals, but in so doing empower panchayats and village communities as a whole. With UNDP we are working on projects which will lead to empowerment in certain specific areas.

As our Secretary, Dr. Saxena mentioned, we are actually sitting right in Delhi, surrounded by an area which is characterised by very low empowerment of women. I feel that some time workshop should be held not in Delhi but in some muddy and slushy village nearby where women view the world through the veil. On a recent visit to Bharatpur I found that women have a very peculiar way of arranging their '*Pallu*' to view the world through one eye. Even though their village may be prosperous, but the income actually does not go to women nor are they aware of the ways in which they can improve the nutritional status of their children. If I were to take a diametrically opposite example of Kerala, you will find that not an inch of land is wasted. Even the fence of the homestead is made of Tapioca. Coconut and banana trees, greens called '*Cheera*' in Malayalam, drum stick trees which are available around the homestead are actually a part and parcel of every day diet. I have had the extreme good fortune of listening Prof. Amartya Sen twice once in Delhi and once in Kerala. On the second occasion there was time even for some interaction and it was noted that women in Kerala are really extraordinary. What one finds is that the child rearing practices and the focus on nutrition is fantastic. I think the mother-daughter tradition based on the matrilocal tradition of Kerala has resulted in much better nutrition of children than would be possible through simple official intervention. A lot of people have taken the credit for the superior health status of Kerala. I think we should humbly acknowledge that it is not so. It is a social practice, it is the traditional practices of women that have actually made all the differences.

A lot of things have been said already and I just want to point out that it is very touching that people realise that despite several disadvantages and several disabilities (it has been pointed out in the document given as background material, that women own not more than 2 per cent on the land) the contributions of women is so enormous in both developed and developing countries. Scientific and technology development in agriculture have in some way marginalised women. I think we have the challenge of bringing them back to the Centre stage and I hope that this particular project in Maharashtra will do so. I also hope that it leads to its replication at several places. I am sure Secretary, Rural Development Maharashtra will manage to take care of any departmental concerns that may arise. We should go fully ahead. I would also recommend that FAO look at the area around Delhi. We can talk to the concerned State Governments and start working particularly on those areas where the very low status of women and children. These are combinations which are visible. There is a casual connection between the two. So if this could be our programme of action, I think it would be really worthwhile. We would be always available for any contribution, because what we are looking for is enlargement of what we are starting as a pilot project and making a success of it. We have chosen Maharashtra for the pilot project because we have great hopes from the State.

I once again thank FAO and IAAS. In fact when we were under training, we use to say IAS stands for, 'I am safe', and IAAS stands for 'I am also safe' so let us not just save ourselves but also help the poor persons to save themselves from hunger and malnutrition.

7

FOOD SECURITY MISSION FOR INDIA

SURESH K. SINHA

Introduction

Food security of the Developing Countries is a matter of concern, and it has been adequately emphasised by the Food and Agriculture Organisation (FAO). However, it is not on the agenda of the industrialised world. I had this realisation when the IPCC special report on the Impact of Climate Change was being finalized. The representatives of the industrialised countries were against inclusion of a reference to the impact of climate change on food security. For them energy, health, sea level rise, recreation, tourism etc. were more important. There is nothing wrong in this and also it is not a matter of complaint. Perception and objectives of the individuals and nations differ, but FAO is credited for bringing both the developing and industrialized countries together on the same platform, and making food security as an important issue of our times. At the World Food Summit (1996) several Head of Governments or Head of the Countries pledged to Rome Declaration on World Food Security. It would be about two years when this commitment was made and an Action Plan was approved. Let us recall the first objective of this Action Plan, because the people of India should know the commitment of our country. It is as follows:

> "The Rome Declaration on World Food Security and the World Food Summit Plan of Action lay the foundations for diverse paths to a common objective – food security, at the individual, household, national, regional and global levels. Food security

exists when all people, at all times, have physical and economic access to sufficient, safe and nutritious food to meet their dietary needs and food preferences for an active and healthy life. In this regard, concerted action at all levels is required. Each nation must adopt a strategy consistent with its resources and capacities to achieve its individual goals and, at the same time, co-operate regionally and internationally in order to organise collective solutions to global issues of food security. In a world of increasingly interlinked institutions, societies and economics, co-ordinated efforts and shared responsibility are essential."

The document identifies (i) poverty eradication and (ii) a peaceful and stable environment in every country as a fundamental condition for the attainment of sustainable food security. The Plan of Action has seven commitments for ensuring food security. There could not be a better document than Rome Declaration on World Food Security and World Food Summit, Plan of Action. While proposing international linkages, it does put a serious emphasis on individual nations. Therefore, we need to consider the issues related to food security in India.

Present Status of Food Security in India

We must analyse the present status of food security in India. There are many who feel that we in India have food security because enough foodgrain is being produced. However, many others feel that this is an attitude of complacency. Furthermore, we need this analysis in view of the following:

- There is an increasing demand of food articles with the increase in population and increasing growth.
- The international trends in foodgrain production, usually a measure of food availability and security, indicates a decline in the rate of foodgrain production.
- It would be difficult to buy from the international market because of both economic and political costs.

Therefore, for a country of the size of India, which does not have oil and coal for export as China, it would be necessary to maintain food security through own production or self-sufficiency. This indeed is important because even the Rome Declaration has emphasised on the nations own efforts. Consequently we must ask the following:

- What would be the demand of food in India, in the next few decades?
- Does the country have the resource base for meeting the demand of food?
- What should be the approach for ensuring food security, assuming that economic growth would help removal of poverty and make physical access of food possible? These are important 'ifs' in this but the country will have to grapple with these 'ifs', and make them a reality.

Food Demand

There have been several efforts to predict the demand of food in future. The International Food Policy Research Institute and FAO using trade models showed that India may not have to import foodgrains even by the year 2020, but the World Watch Institute (WWI) predicted an import of 45 million tonnes by 2030. In fact the latter (WWI) predictions are not based on any scientific analysis, and at best can be described journalistic (see Sinha, 1998). For example, Lester Brown and Hal Kane (1994) of the WWI predict a demand of 267 million tonnes foodgrains and a production of 222 million tonnes by 2030, leaving a deficit of 45 million tonnes foodgrains. They also predict an import of 433 million tonnes by developing countries. Of course they do not say who would produce and supply this much foodgrain at what economic or political cost. China is supposed to import 216 million tonnes of foodgrains by 2030, but the recent Chinese studies have clearly brought out that "Chinese farmers would feed China" in response to "Who will feed China".

Such predictions should not create alarm but help us getting over complacency. There are certain cultural aspects of the Indian society which possibly many investigators cannot appreciate. Some of these are as follows:

- The population growth is now declining and has reached 1.8% or less. This would further decline. The people may be illiterate but even in remote Himachal Pradesh and Arunachal Pradesh they are conscious of population, and its impact on their life and welfare. Many women are coming forward to adopt practices of birth control.
- Culturally India has been a vegetarian society. There is a large percentage of people who do take egg, fish and poultry meat. Has there been any influence of any religion on diet composition in our society? Dr. H. K. Jain, a former Director of the Indian Agricultural Research Institute believes that there has been the impact of Jainism on adoption of vegetarianism in India. He is possibly right. Jainism, though now confined to small pockets, had at one time spread all over the country. They preached that no animal should be killed, and hence they lived on vegetarian food. While the Jainism more or less disapproved but it left a strong impact on the Indian society, the benefits of which we are experiencing today.
- As a religious belief the Hindus don't eat beef (with a minor exception in Kerala and North East) and the Muslims don't eat pork. Therefore, even when the Indian society under the impact of economic growth become non-vegetarian or livestock consumer, it would depend on poultry, eggs, fish, goat meat and milk, the last one being the most acceptable. If for 1 kg production of beef or pork, 7 kg of grains are needed, only 1.5 to 2.0 are needed for other livestock products listed above. Therefore, the Indian society would not have a very high per capita consumption of grains, say it would be only 200 kg annually. Even this may be more, because the direct consumption of grains decreases as the income increases. In substance, many of the projections for India's food demand could hardly be realistic and needs a much better study.
- The above analysis brings out that in future demand of vegetables, fruits, and livestock products would increase at a much higher rate, and that of foodgrains at a much slower

rate. The usual extrapolation of the part trends as the basis of future projections would not capture these objectives. Nevertheless, these changes would demand a major shift in research programme. The new research programmes would have to address the problems of efficient production system of vegetables and fruits and livestock from the point of view of inputs. Could the area under vegetables and fruits be raised to 20 million hectares, with a yield of 20 tonnes per hectare? If this is to be achieved, which land and in which area should be used? How this production can be complemented with livestock production? All this would require intensive research starting from basic to applied. Could we ever think of 1 million hectare of 'greenhouse' or 'polyhouse cultivation'. Each hectare could produce 80 tonnes per hectare of vegetables. What will be the investment in such a venture; and what would be the economics of such a proposal considering region, climate, agro-technology and end uses? The programme would consider pre-harvest and post-harvest storage, transport etc. as important links between production system and utilization.

A Holistic Approach

The national estimates, approaches and aspirations have to be translated and realised at local and farmers level. The leadership can only take policy decisions. Let me use an example. We wish to double productivity in an area which at present has only 1400 kg per hectare rice and 1500 kg per hectare wheat. Firstly, do the natural resources of soil, water and climate have the potential to raise this level. The answer is yes, because it is good alluvial soil, with plenty of surface and ground water, and climate suitable for atleast a kharif and a rabi crop. Then why it is not happening. Could we find an answer to this question from farmers, rather than officials. Some diagnostic surveys have been done in rice-wheat growing regions of the States of UP and Haryana. Have these surveys led to any change and improvement of productivity and production? It is difficult to get an affirmative answer. We, as scientists, feel that the cropping system should be changed. A farmer told an enlightened bureaucrat, "Sahib, you get your regular monthly salary, hence you can advice what you like. But, if our new crop fails what will happen to our children"?

If we realistically look into an agriculture production system even at the best of the place it has involvement of a number of socio-economic and cultural problems to which many scientists, bureaucrats, technical staff and traders in inputs and outputs are either not sensitive or not aware of. Therefore, at every step the question is 'who is the boss'? The farmers might say that they don't get water at the tail-end of the canal, but the Chief Engineer is certain that it is being supplied according to an established time schedule. The agriculture department believes that they are transferring all the advice to farmers according to the scientific recommendations. But the seeds of the varieties farmers get are not recommended for the region, or they even do not germinate properly. The fertilizer supplied to farmers does not seem to respond. If everything goes well and farmers have a bumper harvest, price comes down. Why should a farmer be motivated to produce more?

The point being made here is that agricultural production involves a chain of persons, inputs, monetory, social and cultural, science based technology, storage, transport and marketing for bringing out a change. The combination of science based technology, Government policy, and the urge and adventure of the farmer which made 'Green Revolution' a success story in Punjab and Haryana is not visible in many other parts of the country where exploitation of the potential is just waiting to be taken. That kind of players who made a success of 'Green Revolution' have to emerge on the scene.

Conclusion

The natural resources of India are adequate for food security of the country if they could have an amalgamation of basic and advanced technology and conventional wisdom. The agricultural production system consists of several subsystems and each will have to be addressed for increasing production to meet the growing demands. This is possible if we overcome our scene of complacency.

8

ETERNAL VIGILANCE IS THE PRICE OF FOOD SECURITY

ARBINDA GHOSE

During the concluding celebrations in connection with the Golden Jubilee Year of India's Independence, held in the Central Hall of Parliament and other venues in New Delhi including the Vijay Chowk on the night of August 15, 1998, one of the participants was asked what were the three most significant achievements of India in these fifty years. He placed without even stopping for a second, the Green Revolution in agriculture at the top.

Well, it is true that India which had to import as much as ten million tonnes of wheat in 1967 in order to stave off famine, has now been exporting on a sustained basis rice and sometimes wheat too. It is also true that excepting for a scare in 1966-67, when the country was reeling under the impact of failures of two consecutive monsoons, there has not been any famine as such in India after the Bengal famine of 1943. However, are we really self-sufficient in foodgrains and other agricultural produce, even in 1998? A close look will reveal that there are large chinks in the armour against scarcity conditions, even while the number of mouths to be fed is increasing inexorably at a rate that is alarming, to say the least.

Take the trend of foodgrains production in the last two or three years. In 1994-95, the production was 191.50 million tonnes (mt), which however went down to 180.41 mt in 1995-96. The production of rice, wheat and pulses had suffered during the year, although the south-west monsoon was "normal". Fortunately, in 1996-97, a huge increase of about 4.3 mt in the production in rice and more than 7.20 mt in respect of wheat pushed the total production to 199.32 mt within striking distance of the magic figure of 200 mt.

However, the very next year, 1997-98, saw a decline of more than 5 mt accounted for by the fall in production of wheat by 3 mt, to push down total foodgrains output at 194.10 mt.

The *monsoon* again was "normal" during the year. Of course the south-west monsoon has no role to play during the wheat-growth season. What is worrisome then is that there has been fluctuations in the production of wheat which is grown in areas with assured irrigation facilities and where farm practices are quite advanced such as Punjab, Haryana, Western Uttar Pradesh and Northern Rajasthan. Prolonged cold spell and untimely rains affected production in these areas in the last three to four years.

Then *fertilizers*. Ever since the imbalance in fertilizer application flared up after the decontrol of phosphotic and potassic nutrients in 1992, it has not been possible to restore it all these years. Even in 1998-99, this imbalance is likely to escalate further because of sudden rise in their prices. The "rolling back" of the increase in fertilizer price by the Finance Minister from Rs.1,000 a tonne proposed in the 1998-99 general budget to just zero is not a healthy signal for agriculture, although politicians had their way in Parliament.

The Green Revolution appears to make India smug about one of the most important parameters of agricultural production – *productivity*. Just because some districts (not all) of Punjab have achieved yields of six or even seven tonnes per hectare (t/ha) in wheat and some isolated areas in Andhra Pradesh and Tamil Nadu have registered very high yields of about six t/ha in rice, India appears to consider itself a very advanced agricultural country.

We appear to be blissfully ignorant that a small country like Ireland has the highest per hectare yield in wheat, 8,997 kilograms compared to just about 2,671 kilograms per hectare in India (1996-97). Another small country, Puerto Rico produces 8,333 kg a hectare of paddy. India's yield was 1,879 kg per hectare in 1996-97, Vietnam produces upto 10 tonnes a hectare of hybrid rice and the productivity of most of the foodgrains crops in Egypt is much higher than India.

India, it is claimed, has developed a total *irrigation* potential of about 90 million hectares by the end of the eighth plan period (1996-97). However, except for wheat, the areas under assured irrigation in respect of other crops are dismally low. While land under wheat received assured irrigation to the extent of 85.20 per cent in 1994-95, that under rice received irrigation on 49.90 per cent that year. Only 5.5 per cent of the land under bajra (pearl millet), an important "coarse grain", was irrigated in 1994-95 while its cousin, maize was fortunate enough to have received irrigation on 20.5 per cent of the cropped land. The case of pulses is more pathetic, with the percentage standing at only 12.70 in 1994-95. (Economic Survey, 1997-98).

Then, *per capita net availability of foodgrains* is an important indicator of the nutritional security of the people of the country. The provisional figure for 1997 under this category is 512 grams per day, the highest so far (About 12.50 per cent of the total foodgrains production is set aside for seed, feed and waste in computing the net per capita availability per day). This means that every Indian had physical access to more than half a kilogram of foodgrains per day in 1997. However, the sad fact is that this statement is not true when we consider the parameter of economic access to foodgrains. Various estimates put the number of people in the country going to bed hungry everyday at upto 200 million.

It is on the cards that large-scale *employment opportunities* would be generated in the next few years, which will ensure economic success to foodgrains to a larger population than at present. This will mean higher consumption. However, the total availability is not going up substantially because the target of production for the year 1999-2000 is 210 mt just lonely 10 mt more than what was produced in 1996-97. In the intervening period upto fifty million more mouths will vie for the cake, taking the birth rate at 1.8 per cent and the population at 1000 million (a slight exaggeration over the projected 980 million as of 1997-98).

Thus, despite the spectacular achievements in agriculture in the last 30 years, India is still not out of the woods in respect of ensuring food security to its populace. Threats of floods, droughts, insect and pest attacks, and sudden natural phenomena like cyclones and hailstorms threaten crop production every year. The country has to guard against any violent fluctuations in availability of foodgrains. To quote Dr. M.S. Swaminathan, "Eternal vigilance is the price of food security".

The purpose of this article, however, is not to be little the achievements of India in agriculture. It is now too well known that with an estimated production of 70 mt in 1997-98, India is world's number one milk producer. With 67 to 69 mt of wheat and 81 mt of rice production a year, India is the second largest producer of both these crops, yielding the first place to China, but outstripping the United States in respect of wheat.

In non-foodgrains items too, India has made major advances in the last few decades. Take fish. From just 752,000 tonnes in 1950-51, the production has gone up to 53.48 mt in 1996-97 which is about 750 per cent increase. While only 1,832 million eggs were produced in 1951, that in 1996-97 was a whooping 28,134 million.

In horticulture too India has made tremendous progress and in many articles, this country has attained the top position in production. However, it must also be stated that in respect of prices of two of the most essential vegetables, potatoes and onions, no stability has been achieved, either in respect of production or/and this is more relevant, in prices. Almost alternate-year cycles of high-production-low-prices and low-production-high-prices have been the bane of the potato and onion crops for almost two decades. The year 1998 is one such in which prices of these two basic vegetables have sky rocketted . This, despite the research achievements in developing improved breeds of potato and development of onion varieties which can be grown both during the "rabi" (winter) and "kharif" (summer) seasons.

The flaw lies in less than desired level of development in post harvest management of vegetable crops. Enormous amounts are wasted on the fields, during transportation and in storage. This is one of the weaknesses of Indian agriculture which has to be addressed to in a much more serious manner.

On the other hand, fruits and their storage as also export is a resounding success story. Apples, once consumed only by the affluent and in some cases patients suffering from serious ailments, is now the daily diet of almost every one in the country during the season and even all the year round. Both the traditional and newly developed varieties of mangoes flood the markets during the season. (This year, 1998, was the "off" year for many varieties and hence less availability in the market associated with very high prices).

The same is the case with grapes. Before Independence, grapes used to come either from Kashmir, Afghanistan or the Chaman areas of Baluchistan. Now it is grown in many States. While Maharashtra, Karnataka, Andhra Pradesh and Punjab-Haryana belt have developed grape production in a very big way, one has to mention the success of Maharashtra, particularly the Mahagrape Co-operative, in exporting this delicate fruit to London market for example, replacing to a large extent the Chilean grapes from that market.

No account regarding agricultural development in India in recent years can be complete without describing the fate of cotton farmers of Andhra Pradesh, Karnataka and some other States during 1997-98. India has traditionally been a cotton-growing country because the average people's apparel was and still is, basically cotton-based. India was the first country in the world to have developed the cotton hybrid. The British brought railways in India mainly with a view to exploiting the cotton grown in the Khandesh and Berar (Vidarbha) regions of Maharashtra.

After Independence, cotton spread from its traditional areas of Maharashtra and Gujarat to Karnataka, Tamilnadu, Andhra Pradesh, Rajasthan, Punjab and Haryana. New varieties were developed and there has been manifold increase in its production. (14.25 million bales of 170 kg each in 1996-97). However, during 1997-98, cotton production has taken a nose-dive with production not expected to be higher than 11.40 million bales. The leaf curl disease damaged the cotton crops extensively in the northern States while a major tragedy took place in the southern States, more particularly in Andhra Pradesh.

At the time of sowing of the crop, Andhra Pradesh did not receive adequate monsoon rains. This was the first setback. Then, around October, there were heavy rains in the cotton growing areas of the State and continuous cloud cover for weeks on end. This was the ideal condition for the growth of insect pests. In the case of Andhra Pradesh, the peculiarity was that the pest which proliferated was Spodopters litura which normally attacks the tobacco crop. The farmers were at their wit's end, and rushed to pesticide dealers not only for "advice" but also for loans to buy the heavy doses of pesticides the traders "recommended". Hardly anyone told them that there was a system called IPM (Integrated Pest Management) which would have been much less costly but enormously effective.

The crops were destroyed by the pests, and with that all hopes of the farmers to earn much more than rice would have given them. They had abandoned rice cultivation in order to earn higher return by taking up cotton. As the money-lenders-cum-pesticide dealers turned on the screw for recovery of the loans, farmers found that the only wayout to dodge these traders was to take their own lives. A total of nearly 400 farmers committed suicide in Andhra Pradesh, Karnataka and other States for the same reason.

Reverting back to the question of food security, what is the current scenario and what are the future projections? The leader of the ruling coalition, the Bharatiya Janata Party had projected doubling of foodgrains production within the next ten years in order to ensure food security. However, the coalition in its National Agenda for Governance dropped this ambitious projection and made a more realistic objective of ensuring food security for all within the next five years.

At a recently held one-day workshop on food security, population and environment, various figures were mentioned by speakers. One speaker, the Director General of Indian Council of Agricultural Research (ICAR), Dr. R. S. Paroda felt that the country would require about 300 million tonnes of foodgrains by the year 2025.

Dr. C. H. Hanumantha Rao, a noted economist, was of the view that 300 million tonnes by the year 2020 would be a reasonable figure. However, Professor P.P. Bhalla of the Jawaharlal Nehru University asserted that the demand would go upto 450 million tonnes by 2020 since a large volume of foodgrains would have to be utilised as feed for animals, which were to be slaughtered for meat.

But, then how to increase foodgrains production even by 50 per cent in the next ten or even twenty years? One way would be to extend the Green Revolution to areas not touched yet, such as Bihar, West Bengal, Orissa, Madhya Pradesh, Assam and the other North Eastern States. A less costly alternative is to tackle the low-productivity regime of the rain-fed areas of the country where the average production of the main foodgrain cereals extend between 750 and 1500 kg a hectare and raise it by 50 to 100%. If this is achieved, for which high investments are not necessary, production can go up substantially within a short period.

In its Vision 2020, ICAR has projected, according to Scenario 1, a surplus of 15.50 million tonnes in 2020 on a demand of 324.10 million tonnes. In scenario 2, the gap becomes 23.90 million tonnes on a demand projection of 324.10 million tonnes and production of 300.20 million tonnes.

In either case, one has to draw the conclusion that the Green Revolution has to become Ever-Green Revolution.

9

TOWARDS FOOD INSECURITY

DEVINDER SHARMA

Introduction

Agriculture Minister C. Subramaniam sat huddled with his senior staff. There was tension in the air. Depending upon imported foodgrains coming from 12,000 miles away, and particularly when it came in driblets following US President Lyndon Johnson's directive to " teach India a lesson", was already humiliating enough. What worried Subramaniam was that the food stocks had reached such a precarious low that it was only sufficient to last for another two weeks and still worse, there was nothing in transit. Recalls Subramaniam, " As a last resort, I told my officials and experts to identify the nearest food carrying ships on the ocean throughout the world. I said we would identify the nearest ships carrying wheat to other countries and appeal the US President to divert it to India if other countries could wait for another six to eight weeks".

This was in 1966-67, the critical year of drought when India imported 11 million tonnes of foodgrain. A year earlier, India had imported 10 million tonnes of foodgrain. It was almost at this time the Paddock brothers, often referred to as 'prophets of doom', concluded in their book "Famine 1975" that by the mid-seventies atleast half of India would be led to a slaughter house. Considering that India had a long history of hunger and famine, and the subsequent failure of the government's effort to boost agriculture production in the post-Independence era, not many disagreed with the conclusive analysis drawn by William and Paul Paddock.

Before 1947, Indian history was replete with famines, drought and food shortages. Between 1770 and 1880, as many as 27 food scarcities and famines were recorded. At least 20 million lives were lost in India in about 20 famines that stuck since 1850. Much of it because of the misplaced colonial policies which aimed at deriving maximum economic gains at the cost of human suffering and misery. After the British had created a transport infrastructure in the first half of the nineteenth century, they began encouraging farmers to grow crops which could be exported. The boom in export trade accompanied by rising prices made farmers shift to cash crops like cotton, indigo, poppy and sugarcane. The area under foodgrain subsequently shrank. In other words, efforts to improve agriculture in colonial India was directly linked to the needs of British industries.

In the first half of the 20th century, India's foreign trade showed the same colonial pattern with exports mainly comprising foodgrains and cotton, jute, oilseeds, opium and indigo. Against this, the imports consisted mainly of consumer goods. Meanwhile, the cultivator's preference for commercial crops continued. And as it happens now, the trend during pre-Independence years showed that the best lands available were applied towards the cultivation of commercial crops, while the cultivation of foodgrains was relegated, to some extent, to inferior lands, the yield of which even in normal years is much less. The result was a steady decline in foodgrain output till the Second World War. Per capita availability of food from domestic production too had declined. And as B. M. Bhatia observer in The Famines of India: "India kept the precarious balance between increasing population and declining food production partly by turning from an exporter into a net importer of foodgrains but largely by the easy, though dangerous, expedient of pushing down the already low per capita cereal consumption to still lower levels".

The big gap between minimum requirement and supply had continued throughout the post-war period. Till the 1960s, Indian agriculture was not sufficiently able to meet domestic requirements and the country had to rely on foodgrain imports.

Green Revolution

It was almost at the same time that the Government adopted the US Land Grant model of agricultural research, and agricultural universities – beginning with the Gobind Ballabh Pant University of Agriculture and Technology at Pantnagar in Uttar Pradesh – were gradually set up in all the States. The Land Grand model entitled linking research with extension, taking research from the laboratories to the farms through an extension network linked with the university. And in 1961 the Government launched the Intensive Agriculture District Programme (IADP) to enhance productivity in the irrigated areas. Although the aim was to introduce improved seed along with a package of agronomic practices to take advantage of available irrigation, the programme did not come upto the expectations for want of high-yielding varieties of wheat.

The tall Indian wheat varieties did not provide the economic response to the application of chemical fertilisers and irrigation water, which agricultural scientists were desperately looking for. These had a tendency to fall down or lodge when fertiliser was applied as a result of which the yields stagnated at less than one tonne per hectare. Even though breeding for improved non-lodging wheat varieties was initiated in the fifties, it did not meet with much success.

The missing link was provided by Dr. Norman Borlaug, who was then working with CIMMYT in Mexico. A few dwarf strains of spring wheat that Dr. Borlaug sent to the Indian Agricultural Research Institute at New Delhi, looked impressive. In the next two to three years, a wide range of dwarf material was tested under the All India Wheat Research Project. And in August 1964, the then Professor and Head of the Department of Plant Breeding and Genetics at the IARI, Dr. M.S. Swaminathan, who later emerged as the architect of India's Green Revolution, proposed launching a National Demonstration Programme in farmer's fields, both to verify the results obtained in research plots and to introduce farmers to new opportunities opened up by semi-dwarf varieties of considerably improving the productivity. Says Swaminathan, "When small farmers, who with the help of scientists organised the National Demonstration Programme, harvested over five tonnes of wheat per hectare, its impact on the minds of other farmers was electric. The clamour for seeds began and the area under high yielding varieties rose from four hectares in 1963-64 to over four million hectares in 1971-72. A small government programme became a mass movement." Subsequently the Government imported 18,000 tonnes of semi-dwarf wheat from Mexico in 1966 to be distributed in time for immediate sowing by farmers in the northwestern regions.

The seeds of Green Revolution were, therefore, truly sown in the mid-60s. What followed next is already part of the contemporary history. Wheat production rose to 17 million tonnes in 1968, an increase of five million tonnes over the highest of 12 million tonnes harvested in 1964. Mrs. Indira Gandhi officially recorded the impressive strides in agriculture by releasing a special stamp entitled "Wheat Revolution" in July 1968. The success of wheat was later replicated in rice. And at the same time productivity increase were recorded in cotton, sugarcane, millets and in oilseeds.

Avoiding Famines

The famine-avoidance strategy that India launched had all the necessary ingredients that make for a sustained effort. In 1965, Agricultural Prices Commission was constituted with the basic objective of assuring fair prices for farm produce. The Commission, an autonomous body, works out the cost of cultivation for 22 agricultural commodities, and suggests a price to the government that includes profit that should serve as an incentive to grow more. The administered price of wheat, for instance, was raised by 71 per cent between 1972 and 1981. Similarly, the price of rice was jacked up by 81 per cent during the same period. Later to sustain the tempo of the rice revolution, the relative price structure was moved in its favour. In the early phase of Green Revolution, the price policy favoured wheat, but after the mid seventies it was titled in favour of rice. And for oilseeds and pulses, the reverse was put into action. Relatively high support prices were announced in the early 90s to make their cultivation profitable.

Perhaps the most significant aspect of the price support mechanism has been the insulation of farmers against a decline in prices. Wheat production was very high in 1971-72, as a consequence of which prices should have declined by at least 15 per cent. Since the government purchased all the wheat that was offered, farmers were actually paid seven per cent more. Again in 1982-83, when wheat production was 14.3 per cent higher than the previous year, the prices should have actually declined by 32.5 per cent. But with the government purchasing all the wheat that flowed into the markets, the farmers realised 18 per cent more.

The biggest achievement of the Indian food policy, dependent more and more on buffer stocking and operational stock holding, has been the avoidance of a famine-like conditions. It was with the basic objective of curbing consumption and ensuring an equitable distribution of available food supplies, especially in the deficit areas and among the poorer strata of society, that the Public Distribution System (PDS) was introduced. PDS supplies were also used for the 'food for work' programme as well as other anti-poverty programmes. At present, PDS covers more than 80 million families and the total foodgrains distributed through a network of 40,000 fair price shops accounts for over one-third of the total trade in foodgrains.

Self-Sufficiency

Green Revolution was certainly not a stroke of luck. The resilience was the result of progressive farm policies, determination, sustained efforts of scientists and the vigour of the Indian farmers who readily adopted the improved technology. This is what the Rockefeller Foundation had to say about the magnificent strides taken: "...the speed with which India's farmers and scientists suddenly gave their country an approach to an abundant food supply, has never been duplicated on an equal scale anywhere in the world, including the scientifically sophisticated United States".

Since the early 70s, the country has avoided famines even during adverse weather conditions, through a carefully designed food security system involving the maintenance of both substantial grain reserves and an extensive PDS. The devastating drought of 1987, rated as the most severe of this century, affected nearly 155 million hectares. And yet, no starvation and hunger deaths were reported. This was essentially the result of excellent food management based on the foodgrain reserves built largely from home grown wheat and rice.

From late 60s, the rate of growth in food production generally exceeded the rate of growth of population. Despite the continuous growth in population, the per capita food availability of foodgrains increased from 157 kg a year in 1955 to 177 kg per year in 1995 – an increase of 15.7 per cent. Food production has risen roughly four times since the days of independence, from 50 million tonnes in 1950-51 to reach 198 million tonnes in 1996-97. While at the same time, the population has risen from 300 million to 960 million. Milk production too has risen to 68 million tonnes, the highest in the world. Food self-sufficiency was achieved in late 70s with the maintenance of a sizeable food buffer. Lately, India has begun to export foodgrains about five million tonnes of rice and wheat during the last few years. About 5,000 tonnes of skimmed milk powder has also been exported.

The increase in foodgrains was, however, disproportionate. While the highest rate of growth was achieved in Punjab and Haryana where, at a compound growth rate of 4.63 per cent foodgrain production jumped from 7.23 million tonnes in 1964-65 to reach an all-time high of 30.33 million tonnes in 1995-96. Uttar Pradesh recorded a compound growth rate of 3.01 per cent. Production in Maharashtra, Madhya Pradesh, Bihar, Orissa and the northeast States continues to stagger and depressing. Tamil Nadu and Andhra Pradesh, on the other hand, have recorded significant increase in rice yields, with production rising to 9.17 million tonnes and 11.58 million tonnes, respectively.

The Green Revolution was aimed at the better endowed regions. For millions of farmers languishing in the drylands, constituting more than 70 per cent of the cultivable lands, it continues to be a futile struggle. Despite emphasis on dryland farming during the past several decades, the scenario still remains grim. The undulating topography and the irregular rainfall pattern have combined to aggravate the situation. That the drylands produce about 42 per cent of the country's food shows that the future of farming lies in these areas, nearly 83 per cent of the sorghum, 81 per cent of pulses and 90 per cent of oilseeds grown in the country come from these areas. The poor yields and the fluctuations in production is in itself an indication of the scant attention drylands have received from policy makers and planners.

The problem of increasing productivity of drylands has serious socio-economic implications. With every passing year the gap between the farmer's yields in irrigated areas and in the dry farming region is widening. One year of drought is enough to push a farmer into a deep well of poverty for another 2 to 3 years. And drought is a recurring phenomenon in arid and semi-arid areas. With the result that fifty years after Independence, life for millions of people somehow surviving in the drylands continues to be worse than before. For them it is hoping against hope.

The Decline

The alarm bells have been ringing for quite some time. For nearly a decade, agricultural production had stagnated. The spectacular yield growth recorded in the post-Green Revolution years in Punjab and Haryana have receded into history. Among the multiplicity of problems confronting agriculture, rapid fragmentation of land holdings is keeping pace with increasing population. In 1976-77, the average size of the holdings was estimated at two hectares, and in 1980-81, it came down to 1.8 hectares. Today, it stands at a mere 0.2 hectare. The total number of land holdings in 1981 were around 89 million, today these have crossed 100 million. By the turn of the century, the average land holding will come down to 0.11 hectare. It is quite obvious that with such low land holdings, Indian agriculture cannot adopt the high-tech farm practices.

Basking in the afterglow of the Green Revolution, farming and agriculture have ceased to attract serious attention. In 1995-96, foodgrain production slumped to minus 3.60 per cent, the worst-over since the heady days of Green Revolution. Foodgrain production in the frontline agricultural states of Punjab, Haryana and western Uttar Pradesh, comprising the country's food bowl, has celebrated. The miracle which began with wheat was followed in rice. And this is where the cost-benefit ratio has turned negative. The downward spiral in food production continues through the southern regions of the country. Tamil Nadu, another Green Revolution area, is under tremendous strain from intensive cultivation. In Karnataka, the negative trend in yield levels of all food crops, barring cotton and sugarcane, are all too apparent. Farming in Karnataka can be clearly separated in two distinct classes, the "creamy layer" of corporate agriculture occupying the fertile and irrigated areas and the remaining low productive tracts at the mercy of rains, constituting the tiny and small land holdings. Kerala too, picturesque and verdant with tropical forests, is passing through its worst ever crisis on the food front.

And, as if this is not enough, the number of landless in the rural areas too is multiplying over the past few decades, at an estimated rate of 2 million every year. The rapid expansion in the number of land holdings, with less than a hectare under plough, has meant an additional 6,00,000 farmers every five years or so. The negative terms of trade for agriculture and the declining public sector investments in farming are indices of the sluggishness in this sector. The Economic Survey for 1996-97 has further sounded the warning. The compound growth rate in foodgrain production at 1.7 per cent between 1991 and 1996, is lower than the annual population growth of 1.9 per cent. The survey adds that even a marginal fall of three to four per cent the foodgrains output can cause prices of essential commodities to escalate sharply, necessitating government intervention by way of resorting to imports as in 1993 and again in 1996.

The philosophy of agricultural planning is changing. Gone are the days when the nation's emphasis was solely on attaining self-sufficiency in foodgrain production. Gone are the days when farmers were the newly Independent India's heroes, revered for their role in keeping hunger and sure starvation at bay. Today, at a time when food production struggles to barely keep pace with the burgeoning population growth, farmers are being asked to diversify, produce crops that are suitable for export and to compete in the international market. With promise of cheap food available off the shelf in the global market, the focus has shifted from agriculture to industry, trade and commerce, from the small and marginal farmers to the agri-processing companies which alone can bring in investments and add value to produce.

The restructuring of the Indian economy too has brought the emphasis on agri-exports. Cultivation of staple food is being replaced by cash crops; tomatoes in place of wheat; durum wheat (for bakery purposes) replaces wheat as a staple diet in Punjab and Haryana; flowers in place of rice, and so on. In the coastal areas, private enterprise is taking away the fish catch depriving the local communities of a livelihood and the only nutrition source. In Kerala, vast tracts of forests and paddy fields have been converted into rubber, coffee and coconut plantations. Every year, about 25,000 hectares of good paddy land is being diverted for non-paddy purposes. The structural transformation is not only peculiar to Kerala alone, it is happening in almost all the States. Commercial crops is eating into the fertile land tracts meant for growing essential foodgrains, thereby making the States rely more heavily on the PDS. The diversion of good agricultural land, which in any case is limited to commercial farming and even industries, is further restricting the ability to grow enough foodgrains.

Conclusion

If declining foodgrain production and access to food remain the two biggest problems confronting the country even in the 50th year of Independence, there must be something terribly wrong with the way we look at agriculture and allied activities and an equal percentage of farmers tilling an average of 0.2 hectares of land and somehow surviving against all odds, the time has come to set the balance right. Whether we accept or not, India is gradually moving back to the pre-Green Revolution days of 'ship of mouth' when food was largely imported to feed the hungry mouths. It was the political maturity of the then leadership that led to self-sufficiency on the food front. Few will still question what Jawaharlal Nehru had once said: "Everything else can wait, but not agriculture".

10

EMPOWERING WOMEN FOR HOUSEHOLD FOOD SECURITY

SUSHMA SHARMA

Introduction

The FAO has stated the objective of food security as assuring to all human beings the physical and economic access to basic foods they need. It, therefore, means that household foods security is the ability of the household to achieve sustained access to food of adequate quantity and quality to all household members. Women and children are vulnerable both from the point of view of food as well as nutrition security. The women's food insecurity has three dimensions viz., the inadequate purchasing power, poor literacy and the inadequate food availability within the family unit. In addition they also lack the needed quantity of micronutrients in the diet and safe environmental and sanitary conditions. Thus, it appears that both food and non-food factors assume importance in determining the nutrition security of the above mentioned vulnerable groups. Alternatively, if a shift from food insecure to food secure is to be made, the effort should be to create sufficient conditions for nutrition security and sustained child survival growth and development.

In this chapter, I would like to confine myself to three key determinants namely,

(i) the empowerment of women through education and income generation;
(ii) capacity building; and

The Government of India's food price policy has important implications not only for the nutrition of low income households but also for the real income, since they typically spend 60-80 per cent of the income on food. In India, the share of expenditure on cereals alone for the bottom income groups in rural areas is around 40 per cent and in urban areas about 30 per cent. Also, income and price elasticity for food commodities have been found to vary significantly higher for low income than high income households. It is evident from computations of price elasticities that food price change clearly cause greater adjustments in the consumption pattern of the poor.

Working adults in the labour market compromise to increased survival demands by cutting intakes or alternatively increasing physical labour. The body size and health are affected and they have, therefore, weeded out of the labour market by employing healthier adults from the vast labour pool at low wages. Loss of employment lead to further immerserization of the household. The literature documents that the work loads of women is then brought into severe strain, as they somehow meet the family needs within the resource constraints. They are also required to supplement the household incomes. This makes them even more vulnerable in the labour market, which also makes use of their helplessness. A slow but gradual improvement in the literacy status and development of women's education has made it possible to overcome such disasters by entering into organised work force.

There is a remarkable change currently in the occupational arena in India, particularly in the urban areas where women today are seeking education that would equip them to find jobs outside their homes. Studies have shown that where women control their own earnings employment can increase their voice in the household expenditure. A positive association of women's income and well-being of the children is suggested. Some of the research studies conducted at Lady Irwin College, Delhi have indicated that mother's employment outside the home in organised sector have resulted in adequate availability of food to the family. However, mother's own intake of most of the food items and nutrients have declined, which may be a reflection of time constraint for her own needs. One major effect observed as a result of the mother's work status is the decreased duration of breast feeding in majority of the cases as compared to 4-5 months earlier. A trend towards early weaning is also noticed. These infant feeding practices are coupled with increased dependence on formula milk and commercial weaning preparations. Few studies on status of working women households on the adequacy of diets of their families have shown a positive correlation between the mother's income and caloric intake of pre-schoolers. Female labour force participation by women over 12 years of age is found to contribute significantly to energy intake of young children. Such observations are a pointer to a shift from insecure food households to secure food households as a consequence of the entry of mother into the paid work force.

Since women occupy a crucial role in the management of household responsibilities and are often reluctant to enter into organised sector for work, we have been helping in their capacity building through nutrition and health awareness programmes. This in turn helps them to adopt appropriate child rearing practices in a holistic manner. In addition they are also equipped with skills which will help them to improve their purchasing power.

Women play a major role in overall food system viz., from production to consumption level. They are engaged in all post harvest activities which includes marketing, processing, street vending, purchasing and preparation at home. As such a woman is adept in the traditional post-harvest operations of food commodities and simple home scale methods. Our experience is that simple food industries managed by women can make a substantial contribution to the improvement of household economy and nutritional standards.

Even after 50 years of Independence one hears of children dying of starvation. Often there are reports in newspaper like "160 tribal children died of malnutrition in Maharashtra – the reason being non-availability of food supplement provided by the Government of India" (*The Times of India*, 9th September, 1993). This raises a question as to why one has to depend on welfare schemes for providing adequate amount of food to their children. Infant foods available commercially are expensive and beyond the reach of majority of population from low economic strata. Several researches have shown that one does not require sophisticated foods to prevent such gruesome situations. All that is needed is to give to the child an appropriate solid supplement which is easy to make. Simple 'ready to eat' foods can be prepared by women cooperatives and marketed locally at affordable cost. Production of infant foods in the form of multimixes or ready to eat mixes utilising cereal legume combinations has been found to be successful in several situations. All that is needed is establishment of a small production unit in a village located in any welfare centre. This is an achievable sustainable task directed towards food security of children.

It has been observed that the value of opportunity cost of time, especially for women has important implications for household behaviour. It affects food consumption and nutrition. Even in the poor households, time must be viewed as a scarce resource, not just income. The rising value of time, particularly of women, can help explain some of the shifts in food consumption patterns that are observed in developing countries. In some situations, the shift from traditional foods to more processed, time saving foods can have unfortunate nutritional consequences. The queuing or waiting time also influences the utilisation of welfare services. Thus the household activities performed by women depend on the money, time and services available to them and have repercussions on the nutritional well-being of the family.

Conclusion

In conclusion, women's coping strategies to provide adequate food and nutrition for themselves and their children can be bolstered by empowerment in a holistic manner. Enhancing the capabilities of women through education, capacity building for health and nutrition care and time management will facilitate income generation. Educating women enables them to overcome their cultural norms of self denial and stand up for their health rights, deciding on number of children they would like to have and so on. Access to health clinics will also enable them to take advantage of welfare services available like food supplement, iron and folate tablets, immunisation and nutrition awareness etc. thereby having a direct impact on the nutrition front. Additionally, it will help them to adopt right type of food and dietary practices – a step towards a nutritionally secure household.

11

FOOD AND NUTRITION SECURITY AND WOMEN

KALYAN BAGCHI AND SEEMA PURI

Introduction

Food Security implies a situation where everyone in the country has access at all times to quantity and quality of foods necessary for a healthy life. This, however, is not an easy task, as it involves for a huge country like India, food production at a mega-level, its distribution to all parts of the country, making all individuals capable of purchasing the required quantity, and lastly and more importantly, the actual consumption to maintain nutrition status.

The term food and nutrition security also implies a state of preparedness to face any acute food shortage which would eventually lead to nutrition deprivation of the population, especially of the vulnerable segments. A number of developing countries, with chronic food shortages, developed early warning system to provide advance information of impending food disasters – either man-made or natural.

During subsequent years, the food surveillance system became more refined and was considered as a pre-requisite of food and nutrition security. At the same time, the nutrition surveillance system gradually took shape based on indicators which could be reliably collected from the utmost periphery by workers of different sectors to indicate dietary intake, nutrition status of the vulnerable segments and infant and child feeding practices. Both food security and nutrition security have the same basic objective of assuring adequate food and nutrition to all individuals and to take series of measures to achieve this objective.

Nutrition monitoring is another related term which is quite often used interchangeably with nutrition surveillance. Nutrition monitoring is not a constant watching process like nutrition surveillance, but could be regarded as nutrition surveys done at regular intervals in the same areas, but in actual practice done irregularly due to logistic reasons. However, this procedure gives an idea of the trend in dietary pattern as well as the major features of nutritional status. Nutritional monitoring was initiated in India by the National Nutrition Monitoring Bureau of the Indian Council of Medical Research, which covers presently 10 States and Union Territories in India. Efforts to start a nutrition surveillance system in India are in progress but so far it is in the experimental stage.

All these efforts to ensure food and nutrition security are attempts to keep a close watch on food availability, food intake and nutrition status of the population, especially of the vulnerable segments, in order to take ameliorative action before nutrition deprivation reach a non-reversible stage.

Role of Women

In the midst of this rather intricate process of keeping track of the entire food chain from production in the field to adequate consumption at the household level and thereby to protect and promote nutritional status of the population, women stand out as those who play the most dominant role of a producer of food at the community level, provider of food and nutritional care at the household level, and a reproducer of the foundation of a healthy future generation through their reproductive function.

It is being increasingly realized that women play a very significant role in food production, in processing and even in distribution. Numerous studies have indicated that in most developing countries, including India, excepting ploughing and preparing the soil, most other steps in food production are almost entirely shouldered by women. Starting from harvesting, home processing and even marketing are undertaken by women. In many Asian countries, cooked food vendors are mostly women. In rice consuming regions, pounding and parboiling of paddy is the sole responsibility of women.

It is commonly known that in the agricultural sector, women take the entire responsibility of looking after the livestock and also get food out of these. Major tasks in poultry farming, in dairy farming and in the sale of livestock like poultry and goats are almost entirely carried out by women. The dairy movement in India, in Gujarat which led to the White Revolution has proved conclusively the role of women. A look at the collecting point for milk from the farmers would reveal the large preponderance of women in such an approach.

The tragedy is that there are no official records about how many women are engaged in agricultural work, for how many hours of a day they work in the field, and how much they are paid, if they are paid at all, since most of them work on the lands of their husbands or close relatives.

A most appropriate statement often made is that though millions of women throughout the developing world undertake the major role in food production chain, yet they are the ones who get the least out of food production. Women throughout the world are the major victims of malnutrition. It sounds contradictory but is true based on numerous studies.

Unjustifiable Load on Women

One should, however, notice the big difference between work pattern of rural women and their spouses or other male relatives owning the land. While for male agricultural workers, this is their whole time job of 8-10 hours, for women this is a part of their daily chores. Caring for the family, keeping the household in order, fetching water and fuel sometimes needing hours of trekking on difficult terrain, taking total care of children and other family members, are the entire responsibilities of women. Quite often, she takes up some work outside her home and is paid often in kind, to supplement the resources of the family.

A study conducted by the Indian Council of Medical Research in four regions of India – Chandigarh in the north, Calcutta in the east, Baroda in the west and Coimbatore in the south – revealed the same work pattern of rural women in the agricultural sector. Careful observation methods were used, and time motion assessment was made from which energy cost was computed. It was revealed that on an average an adult rural woman work for 12-16 hours a day, with energy cost of about 2200 kcal or even more a day. Numerous surveys conducted by the National Nutrition Monitoring Bureau and other agencies have confirmed that the daily energy intake is much below the energy output in most regions of the country. No wonder, chronic energy deficiency (CED) is widely prevalent among the rural population and more so among women.

Health of women is of paramount importance in health and nutrition security of general population. Is there any health security of women in India? What is being increasingly realized that there are numerous detrimental factors affecting their health.

Some Social and Health Practices Affecting Health of Rural Women

Numerous studies have been conducted in India, and in other developing countries with similar social and cultural environment, in order to assess the quality of life of millions of rural women and the major determinants. Some of the glaring ones are, mentioned below :

(i) The cultural norm of "women eating last and the least" is common among agricultural population in most developing countries. To some extent, this is based on age-old cultural norm of women effecting their food need when the question of eating is concerned. On the other hand, this can be another example of gender discrimination and through which women are expected to sacrifice their food need for their husbands, in-laws and children. The ultimate result is that women, especially rural women, are the victims of undernutrition and various types of nutritional deficiencies.

(ii) Women throughout India are the victims of iron deficiency anemia, especially when they are either pregnant or lactating. A district-wise compilation made by the

Department of Women and Child Development of the Government of India reveals that atleast 50-70 per cent of all pregnant women in almost all districts in India are anemic and as a result of which they suffer from various disorders which are mostly invisible e.g. being easily fatigued and tired and succumbing to infections of various types. Inspite of such physical state, she continues to be a food producer and home caretaker.

(iii) Far more sinister is the fact that anemia in pregnant women in India accounts for about 20 per cent of all pregnancy related deaths. While child birth is a cause of rejoicing in the developed countries, in India and in most developing countries, the period of pregnancy and the time of confinement causes anxiety and tension in the whole family. Maternal mortality (pregnancy related deaths) in India is today at a high level of 470 per 100,000 live births. Even if she survives the hazards of child birth, with the assistance of elderly relatives or traditional birth attendants, who might be untrained, she delivers an offspring who is already malnourished in the mother's womb with a body weight of less than 2.5 kg. Among these low birth infants, perinatal and neonatal mortality is extremely high and at the same time they have difficulty in later life to acquire their inherited potential.

(iv) The entire life of female in India is punctuated by gender discrimination, starting from her birth as an "unwanted girl" infant due to universal son preference. Differentials in the care and upbringing of sons and daughters reflects the fact that daughters are considered an expensive "economic drains", particularly due to the dowry system. This socio-cultural attitude greatly influences the household, health and nutritional care of girls. As a child she is regarded as a "lesser child", and as an adolescent girl, she drops out from school to serve as a "mother substitute" who incidentally is out of home to work in the field, without any payment as the country's food producer. She is thus an illiterate, and being discriminated in nutrition intake and health care, she is usually an anemic and undernourished. The adolescent girl is prepared to be a "suitable wife" by conceiving early to "prove her fertility" and subsequently being the mother of several closely spaced children even before her full physical and emotional maturation. With each pregnancy, she depletes her body store of nutrients and gets more undernourished. Eventually, she replicates the role of her mother as a 12-16 hours worker – both in and outside her home – at the cost of her own health. Generally speaking, because girls are engaged in more unpaid domestic work than boys, they contribute less visibly to household income and are, therefore "under-valued" and deprived of adequate nutrition. Gender differences continue into adulthood and are magnified in the poverty stricken. In fact, economists, quite often consider poverty as being "faminised".

(v) Almost two-and-half decades of reproductive years of a female is interspersed by a number of pregnancies, many of which lead to abortion and still-births with sometimes fatal complications or with life-long morbidities which they endure in silence. Quite often they are victims of the so-called four toos - "too early, too frequent, too many and too late pregnancies" culminating in a huge load of reproductive health morbidities with disastrous effects on their life.

Women's Development to ensure Nutrition Security

Women ensure nutrition security of their households in two ways. Firstly, they are responsible for food acquisition – from the family farm, through paid agricultural or non-agricultural work; and secondly, they prepare food for consumption by the family members.

Women's decision making powers in terms of purchasing food and disposal of their income along with women's employment emerge as two major aspects in their ability to provide households nutrition security. Their nutrition knowledge and awareness as well as their skills in kitchen management will influence their ability to provide nutritious food to the family.

There is some evidence that women's employment has the potential to benefit household nutrition. However, we need to further investigate whether the relationship is "direct" i.e. due to the increased purchasing power of "indirect" due to an increase in the women's status, and decision making abilities. Further the addition to household nutrition due to women's employment may not completely overshadow the detrimental effects of women's absence from home on child rearing. Some other aspects of women's employment may also influence household nutrition security. In the agriculture sectors the seasonality of employment has a strong influence on household nutrition. The availability of food in the home would greatly vary with the season and the employment opportunities. During peak season, while income and correspondingly food availability would be greater, the burden of work on the women would also be greater, thus influencing her health.

A major influence on health and nutrition status of family is women's education. As child health and survival are enhanced by improved feeding practices, better hygiene and timely medical care, women's education would greatly benefit these. Education also empowers women to take independent decisions. A literate mother will use resources better for her child's welfare.

It is now clearly expected that the most important reason for poor quality of life of millions of women in the underprivileged agricultural sector is possibly their poor health, their wide-spread illiteracy, their low social and economic status, and absence of any decision making even with the family. Such women are completely bypassed either in the development process or in getting the benefits of development process in the country. Nutrition security, the other side of the food security coil is completely dominated by women, and in order to get the full benefit of their contribution they must be empowered to have access to their rights as equal partners of men in the social and economic development of the country.

Conclusion

It can therefore be stated that while a minimum level of income is necessary to ensure households nutrition security, it alone does not guarantee complete protection. Thus, it is of utmost importance to empower women, both in terms of employment and education as a means to improve health and nutrition. About all, health security of women is a vital pre-requisite for food and nutrition security.

12

NUTRITION SECURITY IN INDIA
The Role of Research Institute

SUBHADRA SESHADRI

Introduction

Malnutrition among large sections of the poor in India has impeded economic progress because adequate nutrition is both a means and an outcome of economic development. It is, therefore, not surprising that one of the important objectives of development planning in India has been the gradual reduction and ultimate abolition of malnutrition.

Abolition of malnutrition calls for adequate production of foods to meet the requirements of the population, purchasing power that is commensurate with equitable distribution of foods among different segments and avoidance of loss of foods through improved storage, processing and preservation, such that all households will have adequate quantities of different foods in all seasons of the year and thus ensure nutritional security for all its members. The present situation is, however, far from satisfactory.

The Cause of Nutritional Insecurity

Food production in India, since independence has increased greatly, but this increase has been mostly confined to cereal grain production, through the green revolution. Present estimates of cereal grain production indicate that per capita availability of cereal grains has nearly kept pace with the massive increase in population since the 1950s. However, pulse production has declined and horticulture has received scant attention, thus placing the population at greater nutritional insecurity. Pulses are an important source of protein in the Indian dietary habits and fruits and vegetables are the major sources of several micronutrients.

It is reported that the lowest 30 per cent of the population in India cannot afford adequate calories even if they spent 70 per cent of their income on food needs (Gopalan 1995). Thus poverty and poor purchasing power are major impediments to nutritional security. Considering that cereal grain production has more or less kept pace with the rise in population, the inference is that it is not so much the food production as the food distribution, i.e. inequitable distribution due to poor purchasing power that lies at the root of food insecurity. The current distortion in the distribution of foods among different segments of the population can only be corrected by creating opportunities for income generation for the poor. Although, it is reported that overall economic growth in India has benefited a section of the population and has resulted in an increase in the number of affluent middle classes, the segment of the population below poverty line remains still a formidable 30 per cent of the total. Until such a time that the purchasing power of the poor can be improved, State aided programmes to provide food and nutritional security such as the ICDS, Mid-Day-Meal programme, the nutrient supplementation programmes and the public distribution system for foods and subsidized prices will have to continue.

Despite the fact that India has not paid particular attention to horticultural development in the last five decades, owing to its natural endowment and diversity, the country ranks as the second largest producer of vegetable and third largest producer of fruits (Gopalan 1996). This remarkable position, however, is greatly weakened by the enormous losses and damage to the fruit and vegetable crops after harvesting which occur because of inadequate facilities for storage, processing and preservation, thus depriving the population of a year round access of these foods.

In addition to the above, there are other factors such as unsafe drinking water, poor food sanitation and hygiene, and poor environmental sanitation all of which increase the morbidity burden and result in poor utilization of the nutrients, thus aggravating nutritional insecurity. Yet another critical factor in malnutrition is the lack of knowledge concerning how malnutrition can be averted by relatively simple measures within the existing socio-economic situation.

The Nutritional Problems in India : Present Status

The nutritional problems in India are of two types, arising from inadequate consumption of foods of appropriate kinds (undernutrition) and the other from an excess consumption of certain foods such as fats or highly refined foods. The former affects a vast majority of the underprivileged population in India and is the focus of this chapter.

The four major nutritional problems that continue to plague the poorer population in India are Protein-Energy Malnutrition (PEM), vitamin A deficiency, iron deficiency anemia and iodine deficiency disorders.

PEM is a major cause of growth retardation in children increasing the morbidity and mortality among the under fives. Although severe forms of PEM have declined in India from 15 per cent in 1975 to 5.4 per cent in 1994 (NNMB 1975–78, 1996), moderate forms of malnutrition continue to remain high, with little change being evident (47.5 per cent in 1975–79 and 47.9 per cent in 1994). Thus nearly 50 per cent of children below 5 years are undernourished for want of enough food. It is paradoxical that undernutrition in young children is a common feature even in households where adequate food is available, which is again a reminder that there are other adverse environmental factors coupled with lack of opportunities for education especially for women, that the available food resources are not utilized optimally.

The situation with respect to vitamin A deficiency has improved in India. Nutritional blindness has declined very steeply, while other ocular signs of vitamin A deficiency have decreased substantially from 2 per cent in 1976 to 0.7 per cent in 1990 (WHO 1995). In terms of number of children affected however, vitamin A deficiency continues to be a major public health problem. The long-term solution to this problem of vitamin A deficiency, lies in making available to the population a greater variety of carotene containing foods, which is currently the chief source of vitamin A to a large majority of the population. This would call for not only innovative use of modern technology such as genetic engineering to increase the carotene content of commonly consumed popular plant foods but would also call for identification of all sources of carotene cultivated in India and an analysis of the nutrient and anti-nutrient content of these so that the sources which are high in nutrients and relatively low in antinutrients can be selected for wider cultivation. Low cost technologies such as shade dehydration will also have to be developed to make available year round access to these foods.

The most widespread nutritional deficiency in India today is perhaps iron deficiency anemia which unlike other nutritional problems, creeps in very insidiously but nonetheless is associated with several functional impairment such as reduced productivity, increased instances of infections, impairment in certain mental functions in children and most distressing of all in adverse pregnancy outcomes such as increased incidence of low birth weight and higher maternal mortality. An estimated 50 per cent of India's population is anemic with Hb levels below what is considered to be normal for specific physiological age and sex groups (Seshadri 1997). While the foodbased approaches for elimination of iron deficiency anemia needs to be considered seriously, the low bioavailability of iron in cereal based diets and the relative inaccessibility to foods, especially certain vegetables and fruits that can enhance iron absorption, make it necessary for State aided intervention to provide the iron supplements to high risk groups like pregnant women and young children.

Iodine deficiency disorders have been tackled on a war footing in India. Since iodine content of food is dependent on soil iodine content and in many endemic areas in India, soil is depleted of iodine, salt iodization is the critical measure to ensure adequacy of iodine intake by the population. A recent report indicates that 80-85 per cent of all salt in the market met the standard of 30 ppm iodine (WHO 1993), although we are yet to achieve the goal of virtual elimination of iodine deficiency disorders. On the contrary a disturbing trend is the emergence of new goitre endemic areas in India (Gopalan 1994).

Role of Our Organization in Improving Nutritional Security

The Department of Foods and Nutrition at M.S. University of Baroda is devoted to teaching and research in nutrition with substantial efforts being made to link the two with community outreach. The Department is recognized by WHO as a collaborating centre for nutrition research. The Department is also one of the special assistance centres of University Grants Commission, under which we receive grants for research and updating of teaching in public health nutrition, dietetics and food science.

Our efforts in improving nutritional security are targeted through following channels :

(i) Through developing low cost innovative technology to overcome protein energy malnutrition and vitamin A deficiency. These range from basic laboratory studies to the final step of transfer of technology to the community. The Department studies on Amylase Rich Food (ARF) developed from whole wheat or millets has been extended into the community to make infant weaning foods low in bulk (complementary foods) (Gopaldas 1992). Yet another low cost community level technology that has been developed and tested in the Department is the shade dehydration of green leafy vegetables that are rich sources of B-carotene. Drumstick leaves (*Moringa oleifera*) were found to be the highest in B-carotene with 17.4 mg/100 g. On shade dehydration, preceded by balancing and sulphiting, the leaves retained 50 per cent of their B-carotene at the end of three months of storage, and were found to be highly acceptable in many recipes tested (Seshadri *et. al.* 1997). Thus this inexpensive, easily affordable household and community level of technology provides a means of utilizing some of the currently underutilized plant food sources of micronutrients, thereby having the potential to enhance micronutrient intakes and thus improve nutritional security. Supplementary feeding programmes can make use of such technologies with the participation of the community.

(ii) Through our ongoing research in improving the delivery systems for iron and vitamin A supplements of the national anemia control programme and the massive dose vitamin A prophylaxis programme. Pilot projects that have developed effective delivery of these supplements are integrated into the ongoing programmes with the participation of the implementers.

(iii) Through development of food based approaches (especially iron and vitamin A rich foods) for different segments of the population and promoting them in the community through non-formal education channels to increase the intakes of these nutrients within the existing socio-economic environment. These approaches are targeted to households which have adequate food and yet the vulnerable groups do not receive a fair share of these. Extensive studies undertaken by us have unravelled the various reasons and factors which inhibit the mothers from giving adequate amounts of the available foods to children.

(iv) By developing IEC modules for changing dietary practices and behaviour. These are based on preliminary ethnographic research and are advocated to the larger community.

(v) Through systematic studies of food hygiene and sanitation, especially weaning foods and street foods. The findings are utilized in preparing educational and training materials to improve food hygiene and thereby prevent nutritional losses due to conditions that occur because of poor hygiene.

(vi) Involving programme implementers and policy makers in our efforts so that we are a part of an integrated team and implementation of our research findings can be facilitated. Our organization also networks with voluntary organisations in urban and rural areas in an effort to promote nutritional security, chiefly through education and communication.

(vii) The teaching and training is specifically tailored to develop the expertise needed to achieve the above. There are two streams of B.Sc. programme, one is a B.Sc. in foods and nutrition, the other is a vocational programme of B.Sc. in food science and quality control. While the former provides placement training in government and voluntary organisations the latter provides for on the job training in quality control in industries. There are two streams of M.Sc. programmes which are offered, one in nutrition with an emphasis on public health nutrition and the other in dietetics. Through these programmes, we are developing trained personnel who can contribute in diverse ways towards the promotion of household food and nutritional security.

(viii) Finally our efforts at education in most of our projects is through the existing network of functionaries in the national and regional programmes and are intended to enhance the competence of women and adolescent girls in various aspects related to achieving nutritional security for themselves and for the households. These attempts however, are not confined only to women but include the other members of the household as well.

13

FOOD SECURITY AND NUTRITION IN INDIA

SHASHI PRABHA GUPTA

Introduction

Food Security can be defined as stable food availability at the national, regional and household levels. Thus defined, food security implies a situation where everyone has access, at all times, to the food needed for an active and healthy life. At the household level, food security implies having physical and economic access to foods that are adequate in terms of quantity, quality and affordability. Thus defined, household food security depends on an adequate income and assets, including cultivable land – owned and/or leased – which ensure that each household is able to produce or procure the food it needs. The root cause of household food insecurity is poverty and ignorance.

Present Food Security System

At the time of independence the country faced two major nutritional problems; one was the threat of famine and acute starvation due to lack of national and regional food security systems; the other was chronic under-nutrition due to low dietary intake because of lack of purchasing power among the poorer segments of the population. One of the first efforts of the country was to build up a food security system to ensure that the threat of famine no longer stalks the country. Investment in agriculture and the Green Revolution have ensured that the food production has kept pace with the population growth and by and large India remains self sufficient in food. Establishment of adequate buffer stocks has ensured availability of food stuff within affordable cost even during the times of drought. The fact that the country has not witnessed famine and acute starvation on a massive scale in the last five decades is the most eloquent testimony for the success of these efforts.

Even in the midst of food surpluses, the country has not yet achieved household food security mainly due to poverty, the lack of purchasing power and various other allied factors. It is a matter of concern that even though cereal production has kept pace with the increasing requirements and average per capita intakes of cereal have remained satisfactory, there has been a fall in the per capita consumption of pulses. It is important not only to improve pulse production but also make them available at affordable cost. The production and consumption of vegetables and fruits continue to remain low. Specific efforts to improve production and ensuring access to vegetables at affordable cost can prevent micronutrient deficiency. The achievement of household food security, thus, require inputs from a variety of sectors. In the first instance there must be adequate production of various foods with special emphasis on pulses, coarse grains, oil seeds, milk and milk products, fruits and vegetables rich in B-Carotene (vitamin A), iron, vitamin C etc. These foods must be made available to the people at affordable prices and in remote areas through PDS infrastructure. Further, the people must have the purchasing power to procure the available food. Awareness about right type of foods for meeting the nutritional requirements of different age groups is also essential to enable them to make right choices from the available food. Once the food is procured in the family, the intra-familial distribution among various members belonging to different physiological age groups according to their nutritional needs is also important.

Post harvest technology, building infrastructure to reach perishables to the market are also important issues to take care of the horticultural products. Thus, various sectors like Agriculture, Food, Civil Supplies, Food Processing Industries, Women and Child Development, Rural Development etc. are involved in increasing the production, the availability, the purchasing power, the utilisation and consumption by the most needy age groups.

Some of the key sectors towards achieving household food security could be as under:

Key Sectors for Food Security

Agriculture

- To augment the production of pulses, millets and oil seeds, milk and milk products etc., besides sustaining foodgrain production through measures like multi-crop management, transfer of technology etc.
- To increase the production of fruits and vegetables rich in Vitamin A, iron and Vitamin C through nutrition oriented horticultural activities including home gardening and agricultural extension and to control prices so that these are available at affordable prices.

Food

- To ban the export of pulses, provide foodgrains to common people at affordable prices and build adequate grain storage infrastructures.

Civil Supplies

- To ensure effective and speedy implementation of Revamped Public Distribution System and provide a better package as per the nutritional requirements.

Food Processing Industries

- To promote production of low cost processed nutritious foods.

Rural Development

- To make concerted efforts to improve the purchasing power of the people.

Women and Child Development

To create nutritional awareness among the people through inter-personal as well as mass media approach so as to enable them to make right choices from the available food.

Public Distribution System (PDS) ensuring availability of foodgrains at affordable prices is one of the key elements of the Government's Food Security system. In spite of obvious limitations PDS did play a role in improving regional food security specially in drought prone areas. In an attempt to improve availability of food to population living in most vulnerable areas (remote, tribal and drought-prone regions) the revamped public distribution system gave priority for establishment of PDS in such vulnerable areas. In spite of mounting food subsidies, evaluation studies of PDS has not translated sufficiency in foodgrains to household level food and availability of foodgrains to household level food security. Self-sufficiency of foodgrains at national level and availability of foodgrains at affordable cost at local level to household level food security for the poor, and the targeted public distribution system during the 9th Plan which aims at providing foodgrains at subsidised cost only to people below poverty line are expected to achieve better household food security in families living below poverty line, without substantially increasing foodgrains costs.

Poverty and lack of purchasing power have been identified as two major factors responsible for low dietary intake; low dietary intake and continued heavy physical activity lead to negative energy balance resulting in chronic undernutrition. Chronic undernutrition may be associated with reduction in the work capacity and increased susceptibility to infections. Infections in turn can further worsen the existing undernutrition. Undernutrition and its adverse health consequences are more often seen in pregnant and lactating women, infants and pre-school children.

Bridging the nutritional needs of the vulnerable groups, viz., infants, pre-school children, school children, adolescent, expectant and lactating women by way of supplementary feeding should be viewed as an emergency food requirement since malnutrition is a silent emergency and neglect of the same could push the vulnerable groups into a stage of no return.

Consumer awareness/nutrition education of the people for improving household food security and intra-familial food security deserves a multi-pronged programme for ensuring nutritional security of the individuals. A due place to this important aspect needs to be given in the interest of food security.

The food security would involve access by all to nutritionally adequate as well as "safe food" at all times. Since the increasing urbanisation is leading to an increase in urban population, particularly in the low income group, ensuring the safety of the street foods through various legislative measures as well as training and health check-ups of food handlers has become an absolute necessity.

National Nutrition Policy (1993)

The adoption of the National Nutrition Policy in 1993 by the Government under the aegis of Department of Women & Child Development (as a follow-up to the ICN Declaration on Nutrition) reflects the vision and abiding interest of the planners and the policy makers as well as nutrition scientists in nutritional welfare of the country. The Nutrition Policy recognises nutrition as a multi-sectoral issue and also that nutrition affects development as much as development affects nutrition. The multi-sectoral strategy advocated by the Nutrition Policy highlights the importance of direct nutrition interventions for specially vulnerable groups as well as through various development policy instruments which will create conditions for improved nutrition. The policy has identified key areas for action in various spheres like food production, food supply, education, information, health care, rural development, women and child development, people with special needs, and monitoring and surveillance.

In order to translate the Nutrition Policy into forceful, viable sectoral programmes, a National Plan of Action on Nutrition has been developed and released in April,1995. This comprehensive document encompasses the role of 14 concerned sectors of the Government, like: Agriculture, Food, Education, Civil Supplies,

Health and Family Welfare, Information & Broadcasting, Food Processing Industries, Environment & Forests, Labour, Welfare, Rural and Urban Development and Women & Child Development in achieving the goal of optimum nutrition for the people. The programmatic thrust on nutrition requires a strong interface amongst all these sectors which will receive due attention during the Ninth Five Year Plan period.

Role of Panchayats in Food Security

The involvement of community and the Panchayats in monitoring the services is envisaged through Indira Mahila Yojana (IMY) Scheme. The Scheme aims at organizing women at the grassroot level to facilitate their participation in the existing interventions of the Government. IMY launched in 200 blocks in August 1995, aims at convergence of services of different departments of the government, awareness generation among women and economic empowerment of the women. There will be representation from the local panchayats in IMY groups. The women groups created under IMY would also have a role in formulation of the district level plan reflecting women's priorities.

The Panchayati Raj has tremendous potential for ensuring food security and nutrition. Some of the areas in which the Panchayati Raj could contribute significantly are given as under :

- *Convergence of Services:* Various sectors particularly Agriculture including Horticulture, Food, Civil Supplies, Food Processing Industries, Rural Development, Social Forestry, Women & Child Development, Information & Broadcasting and Health & Family Welfare have a role to play in ensuring food security to the people.
- *Monitoring of various Services:* The Panchayats could play an important role in monitoring some of the vital services like Public Distribution System, Integrated Child Development Services, Reproductive & Child Health Programme – and thus improve the outreach and effectiveness of the same.

- *Nutrition Gardens at the Community Level:* Panchayats could facilitate development of nutrition gardens by integrating the inputs from ICDS and horticulture sectors and thus provide regular supply of fruits and vegetables for supplementary feeding under ICDS as well as for general consumption to the community.
- *Grain Banks:* Panchayats could establish Grain Banks at village level to meet the food requirements during emergency, or special groups like elderly population, handicapped, leprosy patients, vulnerable groups etc.
- *Production of Low Cost Nutritious Foods for Children through Women Groups :* Local women could be organised in groups and given the responsibility of preparing supplementary foods for meeting the needs of ICDS feeding component as well as for sale.
- *Training of Panchayat Members:* This is required to create awareness about the existing services of the government and the role the Panchayats could play in the same.
- *Creating Nutritional Awareness:* Nutrition awareness is pre-requisite for achieving intra-household food security. The Panchayat Members, particularly the women members, need to be adequately trained in basic concepts of food and nutrition so as to enable them to disseminate the same to the community.

Conclusion

In the present age when countries have achieved national food security, and the problem of micronutrient malnutrition is widely prevalent, it is important to ensure a wholesome food for all. In other words, adequacy of foodgrains should not be the only objective since "protective foods" like milk and milk products, fruits and vegetables are equally important for ensuring good health.

14

WATER FOR HUMAN EXISTENCE

K.P.A. MENON

Water is admittedly the source of life on this planet and it could be the destroyer as well. Described as "A Happy Cosmic Accident", Peter Briggs has the following comments to make.

> "WATER is a chemical freak, an absolute necessity, a frightening phenomenon, a benevolent friend. It is abundant, yet frequently scarce. Physically the universal solvent, it at the same time pervades almost all of man's activities – politics, agriculture, industry, forestry, fishing, domestic tranquillity, and foreign affairs. Always utterly essential, water can no longer be taken for granted. Polluted and wasted since mankind took over the world, water is with terrible slowness being acknowledged to require very intelligent handling in the future if our race is to survive.
>
> Whoever mistreats water does so at his own peril. This is as true in New York City as it is in the deserts of the American Southwest, as true in water rich Minnesota as in the cholera-ridden slums of Calcutta. Because the population of the world is wildly increasing, water must be cherished, saved, treated with the reverence some people give only to money.
>
> What most people know about the substance is that they are helpless without it. A person can go without food for a week, but he will die in three days without a drink of water. A city,

it is now realized, can survive patiently overnight without electricity; yet if all the water, including that to hospitals, were cut off for only twelve hours, there would be panic. And it became a distinct possibility for a while that the reservoirs of the largest city in the America would become completely dry."

The Natural Limitation

From the point of view of overall availability there may be no constraint at the moment but it is well to remember that water is not an inexhaustible resource. There is a fixed quantity of this resource on the planet which can be neither increased nor decreased. Does it really mean that a particular point of time, for whatever reason the demand escalates beyond a certain level, it becomes impossible to meet it. Both theoretically, and in fact, it is so, but the demand and the supply of useable water are capable of intelligent manipulation.

The same quantity of useable water available in a particular situation can be put to multiple uses and such multiplier effect, adds to the actual resource availability. Conversely, by more efficient water use and the avoidance of wastage the demand can be brought down as well. All these require imaginative planning and efficient handling.

It has been calculated that out of 40,000 km^3 of water that run off the land and finally reaches the sea every year only 9000 km^3 can be reliably used by the human population. As per F.A.O.'s estimate of 1990 the world's reliable run off provided an average of 1800 m^3 of water per person while the average water consumption per person was about 800 m^3. Though overall availability position should not, under these circumstances cause any concern, this global average has no relevance when we consider the case regionwise or countrywise. There are various regions where the constraint has all along been very severe and the position is becoming worse and worse. The demand for water would go on escalating along with the increase of population and better standards of living. In order to meet the demands of food and energy, careful planning will have to be done even in the regions which do not have the constraint of this resource at present. The correct strategy would be that of decreasing the overall demand by efficient use and increasing the availability to the extent that is possible.

Water for Irrigation

In the developing countries a very high percentage of water is used for agricultural purposes. In order to meet the needs of the fast increasing population more and more areas are being brought under irrigation. India can be taken as a typical case for a case study in this regard because of the variety of agro-climatic regions of this big subcontinent and the varieties of crops that are widely grown. In spite of occasional crisis at different periods agricultural production has, by and large, kept pace with the growth of population. Production of cereals grew from 55 million tonnes in 1950 to a level of 170-175 million tonnes in the course of four decades. During this period and the percentage of irrigated area increased from 17.8 per cent to 34.7 per cent. One cannot imagine what could have happened but for the effective steps taken for augmenting the sources of irrigation during this period.

The country's population had increased from a level of 361 million in the year 1951 to near about 845 millions by 1991, a period of just four decades. While the population increased to 233 per cent the food production had more than trebled during this period. Improved high yielding varieties of seeds and large scale application of chemical fertilizers had, no doubt, played their own roles but could there have been such a tremendous increase had not the production programme been supported by a programme of irrigation of a magnitude not recorded anywhere else in the world during such a short period. At the time of independence the proportion of irrigated land to the total area which was 24 per cent for undivided India shrunk to 19 per cent in the case of Indian Union while it rose to 44 per cent in the case of Pakistan. Population was rising at an alarming rate with an annual increase of 3.96 per cent during the decade ending 1941 which went up to 4.24 per cent in the following decade. It was in this context the first Prime Minister of Independent India, as Chairman of the Planning

Commission started on the venture of a chain of irrigation dams and hydro-projects rightly termed by him as the new temples in the service of humanity. After independence the irrigation potential of the country has increased from 22.6 million hectares at the initiation of the Five Year Plan to 67.90 million hectares by 1985 and to near about 82 million hectares by now.

The impact of irrigation on crop production will be more eloquently demonstrated if we examine the position crop-wise. As already mentioned foodgrains production had increased from 55 million to a level of 170-175 million in the course of four decades. Yield per hectare for foodgrains rose from 553 kg to 1380 kg. In respect of Rice, area under irrigation rose from 32.3 per cent to 45 per cent and the productivity rose from 771 kg per ha to 1750 kg. On the other hand, the spectacular increase in the area of Wheat under Irrigation from 311.5 per cent to 78.4 per cent had the effect of boosting per ha production of this crop from 655 kg (well below that of Rice) to 2300 kg of and above during this period. Even in respect of Coarse Grains a marginal increase of just 1.5 per cent (from 8.5 per cent to 10 per cent) had the effect of more than doubling the production from 433 kg per ha. to 900 kg. Could this increase be attributed primarily to the introduction of hybrid during this period: The answer is an emphatic No. Tamil Nadu where the irrigation coverage for the crop is 9.4 per cent has a productivity level of 1014 kg per ha. Whereas the Punjab yield is 1906 kg which is explained by the much higher irrigation percentage of 60.5 per cent.

In respect of pulses the irrigated area had not shown any increase at all and the productivity is still stagnating at a level of 500 kg. The recent trend of increased production in respect of oilseeds could also be explained by the same factor of irrigation coverage. It increased from 1 per cent to hardly 8 per cent in the course of 25 years but during the following 10 years it jumped to near about 20 per cent of the total cropped area. There was an increase in productivity of near about 50 per cent during the last decade and a half and it is becoming marked in recent years due to greater attention given to irrigation along with agronomic practices. Commercial crops like Cotton and Jute are also showing the same trend.

Potentialities and Constraints

Are we to conclude that the solution to the problem of meeting the ever increasing supply lies in further stepping up these efforts of increasing the area under irrigation? The answer may be in the affirmative to a limited extent only and with a big proviso that water management is much more important than the creation of irrigation potential. Irrigation, while solving a major problem creates in the wake a series of connected problems. The Ganga basin has been one of the well watered and irrigated tracts of alluvial lands comparable to any other region of the world. It has also a history of millenniums of civilization and flourishing agriculture. The same blessing of civilization has turned counterproductive in large areas of this fertile plain where millions of hectares of fertile lands have turned alien primarily due to water logging and bad management of water resources. The new schemes of irrigation in the form of river valley project and big reserves with dams have not been an unmixed blessing. The system of what is known as flood irrigation in most cases has created serious problems for the command areas with excess of water to some areas and inadequate supply to others. Command Area Development Schemes are trying to solve these problems through on-farm development projects like construction of water channels along with scientific drainage system but the progress has been painfully slow. It does not appear that we are able to tap even 5 per cent of the potential for increased production created by the major irrigation schemes.

A few years back, in a national seminar the Secretary incharge of the Ministry of Irrigation made a frank admission. It was natural to expect at least two tonnes of foodgrains from irrigated areas of our country but that was still to be achieved. That speak about the efficiency of water use. A classic instance of uneconomic use of water is the cereal production programme that are being undertaken at ever increasing levels in the desert areas of Rajasthan. The new canal system has made the resources of water available to the people to whom water is gold. If a poor man gets some gold he need not utilise it for jewellry before satisfying hunger. Similar is the case of the agricultural production programmes of the canal areas of

Rajasthan. In a national seminar organised at the Central Arid Zone Research Institute (CAZRI) at Jodhpur it was made out by some one who had an intimate knowledge of Rajasthan – its past and present as well as future prospects – that Rajasthan need not necessarily compete for a high place in wheat production. The State had a great tradition for its cattle wealth and certain other crops. Why should not the scarce resource mobilised at great cost be utilised for getting the maximum wealth rather than spending the bulk of it to get a more limited quantity of wheat at great cost per unit. This point was made out, not by the scientists who were attending in large numbers but by some one connected with the political set-up and the scientists acknowledged the strength contained in the argument. Another example of uneconomic use is that of the summer paddy (Boro) cultivation in West Bengal, a State which had at one time brought about what is known as the Wheat Revolution with more economic use of water. On the other hand their present plan of introducing mustard on large scale substituting the cereal crop of the winter season could be accepted as a step in the right direction.

Sustainability

Sustainable development implies that resources have to be utilized in such a manner that the future generations are not put to any handicap by the steps taken for present development and meeting the current needs. From this point of view it is most important to ensure a proper balance between inflow and the outflow of water. Where there is excess of water in process of irrigation, steps have to be taken either to have a better managed irrigation system or to put the excess water into productive use. For example fishery ponds or tanks for aquaculture could be introduced in such situations. By covering a part of the water-logged areas into fishery ponds the rest of the area could be fit for cultivation with the additional benefit coming from pisciculture. On the other hand, where there is scarcity of resource one could select those crops that require less water. Better attention will have to be given to dryland agriculture. Genotypes that would meet the needs of different situation have to be developed and it should be a continuous process. Certain varieties of mustards are doing extremely well under irrigated condition with high yields of two tonnes and above. Not only that, in their case, irrigation does not require the same quantity of water as required by cereal crops. Even under rainfed conditions there are genotypes capable of yielding one tonne per ha.

Emphasis should be laid on the conjunctive use of water – surface water and underground water. While surface water irrigation raises the water table tube well irrigation undertaken side by side could pump out the water below the ground thereby applying the corrective measure. Where water table is found to be going down progressively caution has to be exercised. One may think of changing the crop pattern by taking to crops that required less water. Simultaneously the scientists may be able to develop certain genotypes whose water requirements may be met before the critical period arrives.

Water for Human Life

So far, we were discussing the problems connected with water for the plants and animals, the water that is indirectly required for sustaining human life. Though required is lesser quantities there is the more essential and vital part that is required for their use directly, all the time. Drinking water has become a serious problem in many parts of the country and the position will go on deteriorating with the ever increasing growth of human population. In large parts of the desert and drought-prone regions cattle go on dying in thousands every year and people have to migrate leaving their homestead behind in search of drinking water. Technology mission for safe drinking water is an open acknowledgement of the seriousness of the problem but one does not get much encouraged by the progress achieved so far. On one hand there is the question of augmenting the resources of the critical areas and making proper arrangements for the drawal and supply. Equal important is the aspect of safety and health hazard. It is very well known that a large number of diseases present in rural areas which turn out to be killer diseases kill poorer sections are transmitted through water. A fully protected drinking water supply system is certainly a far cry but the safety and health aspect has to receive sufficient attention. While the Technology Mission is progressing in adding to the water resources and augmenting the existing supplies. Case studies made during the current year have not given a hopeful picture in this regard. In one of the scarcity areas visited by the present writer with the FAO Representative it was noticed that through the efforts of a NGO the supply of water had been increased by about 50 per cent per through improved methods of collection and preservation.The health hazards aspect had not, however, been given serious consideration. If at all the position could only have become worse because water flowing into the reserve would be carrying pollutants that would not have been there two or three decades ago. As we know, there are cases in which fish living on such water resources have been found to be having toxic substances in their body on being subjected to chemical tests.

Methods of purifying water have been in vogue in our country in the past also. Simple devices have been developed by certain scientific organisations and philanthropic institutions in our country also. Unfortunately these are not becoming widely partly due to paucity of funds. It is most important that the Water Technology Mission should include in fact, not in theory and on paper, the health hazard aspects of drinking water supply programmes.

Conclusion

Water is needed in variable quantities for all varieties of human activities. This Chapter has confined itself to the two important aspects of food and drink – one which requires the maximum quantity and the other which is most vital. In other facets of human activities also water is often becoming a serious constraint as for instance industrial production and proper civic life. Human ingenuity is going to be part of a severe test in this regard and it is hoped that it will prove up to the task. The earlier we become conscious of the impending crisis the better it will be for the up-bringing of future generations.

15

NGO INITIATIVE ON POVERTY ERADICATION AND FOOD SECURITY THROUGH WATER RESOURCE MANAGEMENT

P.V. RAO

BACKGROUND

Indians revered water from ancient times, like the other elements earth, air and fire. Today, in the age of science the respect for water is slowly disappearing, due to indifference, ignorance, and human greed. Precious water is wasted, fouled, and diverted for industrial purposes, thereby denying it to its legitimate use for drinking, food production, personal hygiene, and environmental sanitation. Ecological imbalance due to indiscriminate and massive destruction of forests has resulted in flood and famine. It is, therefore, very important to focus our attention to these serious developments, and educate the public to bring some order out of this chaos. Government alone will not be able to do this successfully. Involvement of NGOs and the Media can play a crucial role in changing the attitude of the people.

MANIPAL INDUSTRIAL TRUST

The Trust was established in 1970 to assist the rural community to organise itself for self help programmes, directed especially towards the weaker sections. The main objectives of the Trust include education, health and eradication of poverty. The activities of the

Trust during the past 26 years covered a wide spectrum such as Literacy, Continuing Education, Development and Welfare of Women and Children, Information Support to Rural Development, Training and Technology Development of SC and ST, Health, Ecology and Environment, Economic Development through Dairy, Self-Employment, Afforestation, Irrigation, Agriculture and Horticulture, Development of Handicrafts, Cattle Development through Cross-breeding, Drinking Water and Environmental Sanitation, Conservation and Protection of Natural Resources, and Human Resource Development.

Major programmes implemented by the Trust for poverty eradication and strengthening food security.

- *Dairy Development Project for Dakshina Kannada District:* In the Co-operative Sector on "Anand Pattern" was organised in early 1970's. Initially 80 village milk co-operatives with about 15,000 members were established and federated into a co-operative milk union. A pasteurisation plant, frozen semen bank, centre for training in artificial insemination and veterinary aid were established. The Milk Union is now operating in about 300 villages in the district and has taken over the Government. Dairy at Mangalore. This Project has been successful in supplying nutritious milk at a reasonable price to the consumers, and has provided a stable market for the rurally produced milk at a remunerative price.
- *Support to Agriculture and Horticulture:* Training and extension support was given to the farmers by our experts and other resource persons in the use of high yielding variety of seeds, use of fertilizers and pesticides, rotation of crops etc., with the object of increasing food production. Uncultivated and barran land was brought under cultivation by implementing lift irrigation schemes at Bailur, Yerlapady, Nabla and Bellur.
- *Afforestation of Wasteland through Women:* The Trust had implemented a social forestry programme in Dakshina Kannada District for about 6 years since 1989. EZE, West

Germany agreed to support an afforestation Programme through women on about 400 hectares of wasteland of SC, ST, Small and Marginal farmers of Udupi and Thirthahalli Taluks. 29 rural women were trained to raise forestry nurseries. 16,69,110 saplings were raised, planted and protected, as against the target of 12,00,000. Farmers with small holdings of 0.5 to 2 hectares of wasteland planted forestry and horticulture saplings. Towards the end of the project the nursery women were given training in converting their nurseries into horticulture and floriculture nursery, so that they can continue to earn a living, when the demand for forestry seedlings comes down.

- *Water Supply and Sanitation Project assisted by World Bank :* The Trust worked as a Consultant to the Government of Karnataka for community participation activities in 3 districts – Dakshina Kannada, Shimoga and Hassan since 1993. 90 villages were selected in Dakshina Kannada, 100 each in Shimoga and Hassan Districts. The community was not involved in other water supply schemes, whereas in this scheme the village community participated in planning, execution, and operation and maintenance. The community also had to contribute a share of the capital cost, and raise sufficient funds to meet the full cost of maintenance. Women participated in large numbers as the project eliminated the hard work involved in carrying water over long distances. Community contribution changed the attitude of the communities towards development programmes, and inculcated in them a sense of participation and ownership. This has resulted in the village communities mobilising the required contribution within the time limit set for them. As the project of this project is to improve the health of the people by providing safe drinking water and environmental sanitation, Drains, Soak Pits, Bathing Cubicles, Dust Bins, Washing Platforms, and Cattle Troughs are also provided. Every household is encouraged to construct a pour flush twin-pit sanitary latrine for their use, for which a suitable subsidy is paid.

Project Details:

Total Estimated Project Cost Rs. 447.2 crores
Duration about 5 years
Project work started in March 1993

12 Districts in Karnataka

Bangalore	D. Kannada	Mysore
Belgaum	Shimoga	Raichur
Bellary	Hassan	Gulbarga
Bidar	Mandya	Tumkur

Total coverage 1200 villages

Phase I : 257 villages
Phase II : 950 villages

	No. of Villages	Population	Households
Dakshina Kannada District	90	3,13,302	60.907
Shimoga District	100	3,39,052	52.813
Hassan District	100	2,05,313	45,141

Objectives

The main objective of the Project is to raise the standard of living of rural areas through improved health and productivity, which would result from improved access to potable water supply systems and environmental sanitation facilities. The improvement of health and productivity would be achieved through the following measures:

- more equitable distribution of safe water
- improved reliability of water supply and drainage schemes
- increased public and private investment in environmental sanitation
- greater community awareness of the causes of water related health problems and the need for a cleaner environment.

Project Components

The broad components of the project are:

(i) rural water supply
(ii) environmental sanitation programme
(iii) health communications programme
(iv) institutional strengthening.

Rural Water Supply

This component is the largest in terms of investment costs (about 60 per cent of the total project cost of Rs. 447.20 crore)

A typical scheme consists of :

- ground water wells with submersible pumps
- a rising main
- water storage facilities
- distribution system
- public stand posts (for about 65 per cent of the population)
- house connections (for about 35 per cent of the population) and
- drilling of wells and hand pumps.

This component would also include leak detection survey and leak repair works of the existing water supply systems and another programme to strengthen the water quality monitoring and surveillance system in rural areas. This component also envisages to undertake measures which benefit water recharge.

Environmental Sanitation

This component is somewhat smaller in terms of investment costs (25% of the total project cost). This, with the health communications component, would have the objectives of developing new strategies to increase demand and usage, and to implement these strategies through innovative programmes in a flexible manner.
This component includes:

- surface drains for sullage
- bathing cubicles
- sink and soak pits
- cattle troughs

- washing platforms
- dust bins
- individual latrines
- reprofiling of road and bylanes.

The village community has to contribute 30 per cent of the total cost of Environment Sanitation and Habitat Development (ES & HD) component. The remaining 70 per cent of the cost is borne by the government. These components will include reprofiling of roads and by-lanes, sullage drainage, bathing cubicles, sink and soak pits, whereas the capital cost of water supply, cattle troughs, dust bins, washing platforms is entirely borne by the government.

Latrines

For the latrines, the subsidies are provided as follows:

Rs.1650 for SC/ST and other weaker sections, and
Rs.1200 for others.

Health Communication Programme

The component is the smallest in terms of investment costs. It constitutes one of the most important activities required to meet the project objective of improving health conditions. This component has four main objectives:

(a) to promote personal and family hygiene;
(b) to promote latrine usage;
(c) to create greater consumer awareness of the requirements and importance of operations and maintenance of water supply schemes;
(d) to create greater community awareness of their responsibility for maintaining the drains.

Institutional Strengthening

This consists of four sub-components:

(a) project management

(b) community participation
(c) training
(d) strengthening the concerned Government Departments.

Role of NGO

- Brief the concerned Government Officials and Community Leaders and secure their co-operation.
- Motivate the required village data.
- Collect the information about the existing arrangements for drinking water, their adequacy and problems if any, and assess the needs of the community and discuss the matter with the State Level Design Consultant, and the Executive Engineer, World Bank Cell and co-operate with them in preparing the designs, plans and estimates.
- Arrange for the constitution of the Village Water Supply and Sanitation Committee.
- Discuss with the beneficiaries and agree upon their share of contribution and ways and means of collecting funds.
- Arrange for the signing of the Agreement by the Water Supply and Sanitation Committee with the Government for taking up responsibilities for Operation and Maintenance of the facility created.
- Follow up with the Committees in mobilisation of community contribution.
- Help the Water Supply Committee to fix and collect the Water rates.
- Co-ordinate the implementation of Operation and Maintenance activities.
- Motivate the Water Supply Committees to actively participate in the Implementation and Operation and Maintenance of the Environment Sanitation Works.
- Maintain contact with the Water Supply Committees.
- Submit the required Reports and Returns to the Government.

Role of the Community

- Collect the statistics required for planning the project.

- Decide on the manner in which the cost sharing is to be done, and the method of collecting funds including water rates.
- Maintain contact with the community members and secure their co-operation for protecting the assets created under this project.
- Maintain contact with the local organisations such as Women's Association, Youth Association and Religious Institutions, and get their co-operation and participation. In addition, organise training for members of such organisations.
- Ensure high standard of construction.
- Maintain regular and satisfactory supply of water.

Present Status

- The Planning process using Participatory Rural Appraisal (PRA) methodology has been completed in all the villages.
- The Village Communities have mobilised Rs.135.72 lakhs in Dakshina Kannada, Shimoga, Hassan Districts.
- Water Supply Civil works and Environment Sanitation works. The systems have been tested and commissioned in 10 pilot villages. The Water Supply and Sanitation Committees of the respective villages have taken over the responsibilities of operation and maintenance in these villages.
- The civil works of water supply and sanitation are nearing completion in about 200 villages, and it is planned to hand over the management of the systems in these villages to the Water Supply and Sanitation Committees within the next few months.
- Tenders have been invited for the remaining villages for water supply civil works. Contracts have been awarded for some packages, and it is planned to complete the process within a few weeks. The target for completing the civil works and handing over the systems to the Water Supply and Sanitation Committees for management in June 1999.

– 5,954 Individual Sanitary Latrines of approved design (Pour-Flush, Twin-pit) have been constructed.

District released	No.Villages	No. of Latrines	Subsidy
Dakshina Kannada	31	3117	2983
Shimoga	21	2691	1761
Hassan	09	86	–
TOTAL	61	5894	4744

Women's Participation

The level of participation by women was high particularly in Dakshina Kannada District where women's literacy is high.

SC/ST Participation

They were keen in knowing the details of the project, and therefore, attendance in Gramsabhas and Planning Exercises was good, because in the existing social set-up they face a lot of problems in getting water even from public wells. However, financial participation by them was of low level because of poverty.

Operation and Maintenance

In the 10 pilot villages in which the project was handed over to the Water Supply and Sanitation Committees about a year ago the functioning is smooth. There were no serious problems. However collection of water tariff from the users of public taps was unsatisfactory. This is made up by collections from those having private household connections. No difficulty was encountered for payment of electricity bills, wages of staff and consumables. There were no major breakdowns.

Guidelines for Operation and Maintenance have been drafted by a Committee constituted by the Government (under the convenorship of P.V. Rao) and is awaiting the approval of the Government of Karnataka. Adequate copies will be printed and supplied to all the functionaries.

Operation and Maintenance training has been conducted in the villages where the water supply and sanitation components are nearing completion. Experience shows that training in operation and training is a continuous process.

Sustainability

The project is need based. The public get safe water at their door steps. People feel that it is their project, as against the other government projects in which they do not have any stake. Financial participation makes this feeling even stronger. The present indications show that the project will be managed by the people efficiently, and that they are willing to raise adequate funds to make it viable. Long term sustainability is therefore assured.

Lessons Learnt

The policy of utilising the services of NGOs for involving the village communities in the process of planning, implementation, and management has paid rich dividends. The communities normally hesitate to bring the problems to the notice of Government Officials. However, in this project, they readily interact with the NGOs which results in quick action. The system of discussing the problems at the village level, district level and the State level in the monthly meetings helps in taking quick decisions, and avoids unnecessary delays.

Attitudinal Change

Even after 50 years of independence, the people have not learnt to regard Government as their own, and public property as their property, and prevent damage to such property. Because of financial participation and the complete responsibility for management of this project, there has been a considerable change in the attitude of the people. The concept of Government being a "provider" is gradually changing to that of a "facilitator".

16

TOWARDS INDIA'S FOOD AND NUTRITION SECURITY

C. GOPALAN

INTRODUCTION

During the last few decades, there have been some significant gains with respect to the nutritional status of India's population. Acute large-scale famines which used to occur with distressing periodicity till the forties of this century have now been eliminated, thanks to: (a) increased food availability at the overall national level; early warning systems facilitating rapid transport of foodgrains to needy areas, and, more than all to, (b) an alert administration and press. Acute food shortages in pockets of distress caused by natural disasters are now being handled more efficiently.

The population of India had increased from 442.3 million in 1960 to 884.4 million in 1992. Foodgrain production had nearly kept pace with population growth; and as a result per capita foodgrain availability had not declined. The prophecies of gloom of the sixties were fortunately belied, thanks to the timely advent of the Green Revolution.

However, while average per capita foodgrain availability now nearly corresponds to per caput requirements, in view of gross inequities with regard to food distribution, a large proportion of poor households do not have access to adequate food. We are, therefore, witness to the cruel paradox of satisfactory buffer stocks

Paper was presented at the IAAS-FAO World Food Day Workshop, 1992 in preparation for the International Conference on Nutrition, held at Rome in December 1992.

of foodgrains (reported to be about 37 million tonnes as per the latest estimates) on the one hand, and pockets of undernutrition on the other. India's nutrition problem is thus not so much one of lack of foodgrains at the overall national level, but of lack of adequate access to food in over (at least) 30 per cent of poor households whose family incomes are so low, that even if 70 per cent of that family income is spent on food, nutritional needs are not met. We will return to this aspect later in this Chapter.

FOOD PRODUCTION

Though the situation with respect to foodgrain production seems satisfactory, complacencies may not be warranted, our current huge buffer stocks notwithstanding.

The five major aspects with respect to food production that should demand our attention from the point of national food and nutrition security are:

- (i) correction of prevailing distortions in the pattern of food production;
- (ii) laying the ground work for successful exploitation of the new emerging tools of biotechnology and genetic engineering for optimising our food production capabilities;
- (iii) protection and conservation of our land resources for food production;
- (iv) protection and conservation of our water and marine food resources; and
- (v) improvements in storage, processing and preservation of food and in their quality control.

Pattern of Food Production

Optimal nutrition will demand the intake of a wide range of foods, which taken together and in judicious combination (in a well balanced diet) can provide the essential nutrients that we need. Ensuring good nutrition is not just equivalent to avoidance of hunger. While the latter can be achieved through the intake of a single staple cereal, the former will demand besides cereals, an adequate supply of other foods such as pulses, vegetables and fruits and milk. While, understandably, we may be immediately concerned with efforts to stave off hunger among the poor, our long-term goal must be the achievement of an optimal State of nutrition for our people, which will help them find full expression to their genetic potential. Nutrition security is much more than Food Security; the former will involve our having to broaden and diversify our food base.

The Green Revolution despite its striking success in the matter of augmentation of wheat and rice output had brought about some distortions in the pattern of food production. Two major distortions which are important from the nutrition point of view deserve special attention.

Pulse/legumes production has shown no significant gains, with the result that the per capita availability of pulses has sharply declined and the prices of pulses have escalated to levels beyond the reach of the poor. This is bound to be reflected in a sharp decline in the protein quality of diets in poor households. The answer to this does not consist in fortification of cereals with lysine; but in overcoming current bottlenecks to augmentation of pulse/legume production. Pulses are not merely a good source of lysine (deficient in cereals) but also a good source of riboflavin also generally deficient in predominantly cereal based diets. It must be pointed out that the prevalence of Vitamin B Complex deficiencies (and especially of riboflavin deficiency) in our children and women is high and indeed considerably exceeds the prevalence of vitamin A deficiency. Legume cultivation, as part of crop rotation, is also beneficial to soil.

Horticultural development had also not received adequate attention; and as a result micronutrient deficiencies have now come to the fore. This is sad, considering the country's rich biodiversity and the bewildering varieties of fruits and vegetables that Nature has endowed it with.

New Horizons

New challenges and opportunities for augmenting food production are now unfolding with recent advances in biotechnology and genetic engineering. Given our rich biodiversity, and our large scientific manpower, we are richly endowed with the capabilities to respond to the new challenges. Research designed to identify high nutritive value varieties of fruits and vegetables and genetic engineering with a view to maximise yield and nutritive value of a wide range of foods, will need to be supported. In an earlier publication, I had referred to the several opportunities that the new biotechnologies offer in this regard and I shall not go into further details on this aspect here.

Protection and Conservation of Soils

The use of high analysis chemical fertilizers, which is part of the modern intensive agricultural technology, had not always gone hand in hand with appropriate measures for soil testing and soil replenishment, with the result that, as shown by studies of FAO, there are disturbing evidences of micronutrient depletion of soils in some areas; these are likely to be eventually reflected in impaired nutritive value of foodgrains grown in such soils. Our precious land resources must be preserved and their continued fertility must be ensured.

All this, however, are not arguments against the Green Revolution, as such, which had saved many developing countries, including India, from the prospects of severe food scarcity; rather, they are arguments of institution of appropriate corrective measures to overcome the distortions in the pattern of food production consequent on the new agricultural technologies.

Protection of Marine Food Sources

Industrial plants located in the vicinity of banks of rivers in the country are now discharging effluents containing potentially toxic pollutants, which may be contributing not only to the observed dimunition in fish catches but also to metallic and toxic contamination of fish. A whole array of industries, such as pulp and paper, textiles, tanneries, sugar, distilleries, shellac, hydrogenated vegetable oils, coal washeries and petrochemicals are located on the banks of rivers and streams and are discharging such effluents.

The most notable metallic pollutants derived from such industrial establishments are mercury, lead, chromium, cadmium, copper and zinc. These contaminants are not only likely to persist over a long period but they are also generally water soluble, non-degradable and strongly bonded to polypeptides and proteins. The source of mercury is generally chlor-allkali plants which manufacture chlorine and caustic soda. Mercury is extremely toxic to fish and man.

Lead finds its way into rivers and ponds from the wastes of industries manufacturing storage batteries, cable sheathing, pigments, water pipes etc. Cadmium pollution arises from industries manufacturing kitchen utensils and glazed potteries. Zinc, chromium and copper poisoning arises from effluents of metallic industries, mines and dye industries, and leather and explosive industries. Our impressive reverie and marine food sources should be zealously guarded and protected, and the current degradations must be arrested.

Food Processing, Preservation and Quality Control

At present a considerable part of food produced perish for lack of adequate facilities for storage and good preservation. Fungal contamination of cereals, loss of food through pests and rodents, and wastage of fruits and vegetables currently take a heavy toll. The answer to my mind is not food irradiation, which may sound a 'modern' and scientific approach; but which, in my opinion, is not a desirable procedure atleast as far as staples are concerned. Simple, safe village-based decentralised technologies for preservation and processing of food are already available; and need to be refined, reinforced and propagated. Simple methods of dehydration of vegetables for storage and use in lean seasons will go a long way towards promotion of consumption of green leafy vegetables (GLVs) and fruits and towards combating micronutrient deficiencies. Facilities for collection of vegetables at production points in the villages, for the removal of non-edible portions, for blanching of edible portions and packaging in polythene bags for distributing through a chain of outlets in urban and semi-urban areas will go a long way in reducing the price of vegetables and increasing their consumption. These operations can easily be undertaken by village co-operatives.

With urbanisation and change in occupational pattern, "convenience foods" and ready-to-eat foods will be in increasing demand. Safe and inexpensive indigenous technologies will need to be developed for this purpose. Agro-based industries with large employment potential may need to be developed in order to achieve these objectives. Most importantly, current methods for ensuring quality control of food need to be strengthened and refined.

FOOD DISTRIBUTION

Now to return to the subject of inequitable distributions of food and inadequate access to it on the part of millions of poor households in the country.

The Magnitude of the Problem of Poverty

India's Planning Commission had estimated that in 1987-88, 29.9 per cent of India's population (then numbering 238 million) lived below the 'Poverty line', the poverty line being the expenditure required to acquire the estimated minimum calorie requirement of 2400 Kcals per capita daily in rural areas and 2100 Kcals per capita daily in urban areas. The Expert Committee on Poverty of Planning Commission, on the other hand, using somewhat different yardsticks, had estimated the population of 'poor' in the country to be 39.34 per cent or 31.3 million.

These estimates are based on approximations and assumptions that may be debatable. The expert committee referred to above had also pointed out that there were significant Inter-State differentials with respect to food prices and therefore, with respect to poverty levels. Despite doubts and possible uncertainties, these estimates, from an official committee on the Planning Commission (not a group of "anti-establishment activities") provide a broad indication of the magnitude of poverty in the country. It must, however, be remembered that estimates of 'poverty' need not necessarily be considered as being equivalent to estimates of 'undernutrition'. As Meera Chatterjee points out: "not all who are poor are malnourished; and not all who are malnourished are 'poor'. Perhaps an even more direct indication of the extent of food deprivation may be the observation of expert committee that nearly 19 per cent of rural households, and over 6 per cent of urban households had reported that they were not getting two square meals a day for either part or the whole of the year.

While these findings are depressing there are indications that despite population increase the proportion of population below the 'poverty line' has been declining though not perhaps as rapidly as one would wish. Thus the Expert Committee referred to above and estimated that poverty as per its estimation, had declined from 55 per cent in 1973-74 to 39 per cent in 1987-88.

While there may have been no spectacular decline in overall poverty, disaggregated data on family income levels in poor income groups as reported by NNMB, seem to indicate that 'abject poverty' may have declined as reflected in a shrinkage in the proportion of population with the lowest (of low) income levels.

The fact that there has been a near-total disappearance of fluoride manifestations of undernutrition like classical kwashiorkor and Keratomalacia, Beri-Beri and pellagra which were once major public-health problems in some parts of the country would support the conclusion that there has been a decline in abject poverty. The periodic surveys carried out by the National Nutrition Monitoring Bureau show that "severe malnutrition" in under-fives as reflected in weight/age less than 60 per cent of standard has also significantly declined.

While these gains are gratifying, the fact remains that the country has still a long way to go before it can be legitimately claimed that adequate progress towards eradication of unequities has been achieved. Recent gains that may have accrued at the macroeconomic level through policies of globalisation and 'liberalisation' have yet to be significantly reflected in better nutritional status of the poor. The "trickle down effect" is not as yet manifest and perhaps, it is too soon to expect such results. Apparently there are still quite a few blocks in the 'conduit' from the top to the bottom. "Lateral inputs" in the form of welfare measures now being resorted to are, therefore, necessary at least in the immediate present. However, such measures while being welcome, are of the nature of "relief and repair operations" and cannot be the final answer. The final answer must lie in ensuring for even poor households, income levels adequate to meet their basic minimal requirements for food, clothing and shelter. This challenge cannot be evaded and there are no short-cuts. "The Right to Food, Clothing and Shelter" is perhaps the most important of all Humane Rights, being related to Human Survival itself.

Anti-Poverty Programmes

In this context, the ongoing anti-poverty and welfare programmes, such as ICDS, and the more recent ones such as the Mid-day Meal programme in schools, are important initiatives; but their efficacy in alleviating undernutrition even in the short run will very much depend on how well these programmes are targeted to benefit the really needy groups, and how efficiently (and honestly) they are implemented. The recent bold initiatives towards decentralisation of administration, through the creation of elected empowered village panchayats all over the country with 30 per cent of the elected seats reserved for women, may help ensure that the benefits of the welfare programmes really reach the poor.

The Public Distribution System

A major instrument for ensuring equity in the matter of food distribution is the Public Distribution System (PDS). In a recent masterly analysis of this system, Venugopal drew attention to some of the glaring deficiencies in the system. He argued that the prevailing agricultural and food pricing policies may have contributed to the observed progressive decline in the off-take of foodgrains from the fair price shops of the PDS during recent years. A good part of central food subsidies, according to him benefit the farmer and go to meet the management costs of buffer-stocks, rather than to benefit the consumer. The consumption of cereals, as estimated by the National Sample Survey, 48th round of 1994, had declined from 14.4 kg in 1987-88 to 13.5 kg in 1992. The off-take of foodgrains through PDS had declined from 16.64 million tonnes to 12.57 million tonnes in 1994-95. It is hoped that the 'revamping' of PDS initiated in 1992-93 will yield results in due course.

In view of these disturbing trends, there is clearly a need to look deeply into ways of improving the PDS so as to ensure that its benefits are targeted to the poor and needy. In order to do this we need to have reliable data on the profile of the present users of PDS, of the relative off-take different foods offered through the system, and of possible factors contributing to the poor utilisation of this service – data of the type which Venugopal himself had collected for Andhra Pradesh.

Among the many possible explanations for the poor off-take of foodgrains through the PDS, apart from the reasons suggested by Venugopal, there is also a possibility that a good proportion of the "non-poor" who were earlier availing themselves (needlessly) of the PDS facility, have now stopped doing so finding that the price differential between the PDS and the open market is not all that attractive. Should this be the case, it could turn out that the poorer off-take may actually indicate better targeting (however unintentioned).

In this connection it must be pointed out that while the benefits of recent globalisation and liberalisation initiatives have still to become manifest as far as the poor are concerned, there has been a rapid expansion of the ranks of affluent middle-class. While precise estimates are hard to come by, it has been suggested that the affluent middle class may number over 200 million. It is possible that many of these were once users of the PDS but not now. It is to be hoped that the expansion of the middle-class is an early manifestation of the trickle down effect and will be reflected in due course in a progressive shrinkage of the ranks of the poverty stricken in the country.

There is yet another aspect that needs to be considered in considering the data reflecting poor off-take from PDS. It must be pointed out that even the highest level of off-take of foodgrains from the PDS at any time, represented only a small fraction of the total foodgrains that must have been consumed by the poor. This will be evident from a simple arithmetic calculation based on SRS data regarding average daily per capita intake of foodgrains, and the estimates of the total population below the poverty line. Since it may be unreasonable to assume that the poor prefer the (marginally) more expensive open market to PDS, it may seem logical to conclude that a large proportion of the poor – made up of agricultural labourers and small land holders – are "eating off the land", and their food consumption figures are not reflected in market transactions. Under the circumstances it may be practical and prudent to strengthen and provide support to the prevailing (off-market or non-market) practices that the poor have traditionally evolved and which they are currently practicing for meeting their food needs and their survival.

It must be said in conclusion, that the durable way of ensuring adequate food supplies to poor households will be not through hand-outs and welfare operations but through improving the capacity of the poor to earn their livelihood with dignity. This implies that the quality of human resource, represented by these households, will need to be improved through better health care and education. Again, as Meera Chatterjee points out "improving nutrition cannot be relegated to welfare or populist philanthropy". It is the very essence of the development.

NUTRITION AND NATIONAL DEVELOPMENT

The mutually synergistic interrelationship between improvement of nutritional status of a population and its overall socio-economic development is now well recognised. Optimal nutritional status is at once a means and the outcome of socio-economic development. Nutrition upliftment programmes must therefore be considered in the total context of socio-economic development.

Human Development Index

International agencies have attempted to evolve a "Human Development Index" which takes note of both economic status (as indicated by GDP) and social development (as indicated by educational attainment and health status); and on the basis of this index they have attempted to rank countries in the order of development. India figures among the "Low Development" countries in this classification. Of all the 174 nations of the world listed in this exercise, India has been placed as 134th . This exercise has its obvious imperfections and limitations; but all the same provides a rough measure, albeit of debatable validity, of the order of development/under-development. More importantly it reveals the persisting developmental gap as between the countries of Europe and North America on the one hand, and developing countries on the other, and thus provides a strong indictment of prevailing inequities in the World Economic Order (disorder).

The National Nutrition Scenario

We will here attempt to briefly review the national nutrition scene in the context of overall social development. India is a vast country with marked inter-regional and intra-regional variations. An "average developmental index" for the entire country will have little meaning and will provide no practical leads for action. We must atleast be able to look at the different States of the Indian Union individually.

There have been several small scale/surveys of health/nutrition in the country but the data from these may not be representative of the country as a whole. The two major national surveys which provide data related to nutrition covering large sections of the country's population are: (1) The surveys carried out by the National Nutrition Monitoring Bureau (NNMB) of the National Institute of Nutrition, Hyderabad, and (2) The recent National Family Health Survey (NFHS). The data derived from these surveys have their limitations and are not strictly comparable. The NNMB surveys cover only 8 States of the country and the latest data pertain to 1991. The NFHS covers a much wider area but the emphasis here being on reproductive health, data related to nutrition are somewhat limited. The National Sample Survey in its several rounds collects data on food expenditure but these are not recent.

Apart from the above, the Indian Council of Medical Research has carried out large-scale countrywide studies on maternal and infant nutrition and findings of these studies have been presented in important reports. An attempt has been made in this Chapter to rank different States of the Indian union on the basis of such criteria as: (a) life expectancy; (b) 'knowledge' as reflected by literacy level and years of schooling; and (c) nutritional status of the under-fives. This categorisation does not take into account the 'economic development' criterion for each State as this is difficult to determine with reasonable precision. Besides this, this exercise attempted here has several other limitations. Even so, it may provide some measures of the prevailing order of social development and of the profile of health/nutrition status of different States of the country. It must however be remembered that within each State, (intra-State) inequities are often glaring and the order of intra-State inequities may differ, as between different States. As such "average figures" for a whole State may not reflect a true picture. These possibilities are fully recognised.

For the purpose of the present analysis of the latest available information on national nutritional status, the data from the NNMB and NFHS have been used. A detailed critical analysis of all these data is being undertaken by the Nutrition Foundation of India and the results thereof will be reported separately in a special publication of the Foundation later. Only a few brief comments are presented here.

Data from the NNMB Surveys

NNMB had brought out two valuable reports containing the results of its surveys at two points of time 1974–79 and 1988–90. The computation of undernutrition in children using anthropometric indices had been earlier carried out using the conventional IAP (Indian Academy of Paediatrics) system of classification wherein the degree of undernutrition (deficits in weight for age) was expressed in terms of percentage of the median standard. In line with more recent practice, NNMB has now reanalysed its raw data and has now converted these original computations in terms of percentage of children with weight/age falling below either <–2SD or <–3SD of the standard (Z score system).

The values for percentage of children with weight for age falling below <–3SD are bound to be significantly higher than the estimates of "severe undernutrition" arrived at with the use of the earlier 'IAP' approach wherein weight/age deficits were expressed as percentage of the standard (< 60%); the cut-off points in the two approaches are different and the estimates, therefore, are not comparable. Failure to understand this significant difference in estimates arrived at by the two different approaches may lead to the erroneous and alarming inference that 'severe malnutrition' in children in the country has increased (which certainly is not the case).

The NNMB data from the two surveys pertaining to 8 States of the Indian Union have been indicated in Tables 16.1 and 16.2. The States covered in the survey have been 'ranked' 1 to 8, (the best being 1 and the worst 8) with respect to 'nutritional status' as measured by the prevalence of under-nutrition in children and "food consumption" as measured by calorie intake per consumption. Some of the salient findings may be summarised as follows:

(a) The most recent survey report (1988-90) indicates that between 42.5 per cent under fives (in Kerala) and 69.5 per cent (in Orissa) could be considered as undernourished using the <–2SD of median (Z score) criterion; between 11.8 per cent (in Kerala) and 41.8 per cent (in Madhya Pradesh) were below –3SD.

(b) There has been a significant decline in the prevalence of undernutrition in children in all but one State (Orissa) between 1979 and 1989 – a ten year period, the decline being most striking in Kerala and least striking in Madhya Pradesh. The situation in Orissa in 1989 was actually worse than in 1979.

(c) The prevalence of 'severe malnutrition' was marginally higher in girls than in boys in all States surveyed (Table 16.2). The rather curious and inexplicable finding was that the increase in the prevalence of 'severe malnutrition' in girls as compared to boys was marked in Kerala State considered to be the most (socially) progressive. On the other hand, when prevalence of all grades of malnutrition (including mild, moderate and severe <–2SD) was considered as a whole, the girls were generally better off than boys in all States (including Kerala) except Orissa. This would suggest that the neglect of the girl child is probably more with respect to the promptness with which medical attention is sought during illnesses (which generally tend to convert 'moderate' malnutrition into the severe form), rather than in the matter of general sharing of the family food pot as between boys and girls.

(d) A striking finding was the lack of parallelism between average household calorie and protein consumption in a given State on the one hand, and the prevalence of undernutrition in its children on the other. Thus the State which showed the best record (the lowest prevalence) with respect to undernutrition in children, namely Kerala, was the poorest with respect to the household food consumption; per centre, the State with a fairly poor record with respect to prevalence of undernutrition in children (Madhya Pradesh) showed the best figures for household food consumption (Figures for household food consumption from Orissa were not available). This would suggest either: (a) that intrafamilial distribution of food was more unfavourable with respect to children in States like Madhya Pradesh as compared to Kerala; or (b) that infections which contribute to malnutrition are more promptly and efficiently combated in a State like Kerala with better health care system than in States like with poorer health-care system. Moreover "average" figures of consumption may not necessarily reflect consumption; the distribution of consumption data may perhaps reflect a better picture.

(e) There is a direct relationship between the level of energy consumption and protein consumption. This is to be expected considering that the main source of calories and of protein is nearly the same – being a single staple cereal with insignificant amounts of fat (calorie rich) and protein-rich foods like pulses or meat.

Table16.1: Ranking of States According to Nutritional Status and Energy Consumption.

(NNMB data, 1988-90 and 1974-79)

State	Ranking acc. to Nutritional Status	Nutritional Status of children < 4 yrs(%)		Ranking acc. to Energy Consump-tion	Avg. Consumption of Nutrients (Cu/day) (at house-hold level)	
		<–2SD	<–3SD		Energy (Kcal)	Protein (g)
Kerala	1	42.5	11.8	6	2140	52.9
	(1)	(61.2)	(28.9)	(7)	(1978)	(46.4)
Tamil Nadu	2	56.6	22.6	7	1871	45.6
	(3)	(66.3)	(34.7)	(5)	(2275)	(54.8)
Maharashtra	3	60.1	24.0	5	2211	61.7
	(7)	(72.8)	(40.6)	(3)	(2300)	(64.5)
Andhra Pradesh	4	60.7	28.4	4	2340	55.7
	(4)	(66.9)	(35.6)	(2)	(2447)	(59.8)
Karnataka	5	65.9	31.3	2	2431	65.4
	(6)	(71.6)	(36.4)	(1)	(2932)	(79.3)
Gujarat	6	67.2	36.9	3	2375	69.3
	(8)	(74.4)	(43.4)	(6)	(2162)	(64.2)
Madhya Pradesh	7	68.9	41.8	1	2614	82.5
	(5)	(70.8)	(41.3)	(4)	(2283)	(71.5)
Orissa	8	69.5	35.7	–	–	–
	(2)	(33.2)	(33.2)	–	–	–

Note: Figures in parentheses correspond to 1974-79 values.
Rank of the State with lowest % of under-nutrition = 1.
Rank of the State with highest level of energy consumption = 1.

The NFHS Data and the Index of Nutrition and Social Development (INSD)

The NFHS data do not provide information on food consumption but include figures regarding child mortality rates. Using NFHS data an attempt has been made to evolve an Index of Nutrition and Social Development (INSD) with respect to different States (Table 16.3). The statistical note prepared by M. K. Rai, statistician at NFI on INSD is provided in Annexure 1.

Table 16.2 : Gender Difference in Child Nutrition Percent Distribution of Boys and Girls Under Four Years according to Nutritional Status (NNMB - 1988-90 and 1974-79)

State	Nutritional Status (Weight-for-age)			
	<–3SD		<–2SD	
	Male	Female	Male	Female
Andhra Pradesh	27.2	29.8	61.3	60.2
	(36.4)	(34.7)	(68.4)	(65.4)
Gujarat	36.0	37.7	67.4	67.3
	(39.9)	(47.5)	(74.9)	(73.9)
Karnataka	31.0	31.6	64.4	67.5
	(33.3)	(39.7)	(71.3)	(71.9)
Kerala	9.3	14.8	47.1	38.6
	(27.1)	(30.6)	(63.1)	(59.3)
Madhya Pradesh	41.3	43.1	72.0	67.8
	(39.4)	(43.1)	(71.3)	(70.1)
Maharashtra	20.6	27.2	60.0	60.1
	(38.4)	(42.9)	(73.9)	(71.2)
Orissa	30.5	40.7	65.4	73.2
	(30.4)	(36.6)	(62.9)	(62.0)
Tamil Nadu	19.1	26.3	56.1	57.0
	(33.4)	(35.9)	(64.6)	(68.1)

Note: Figures in parentheses correspond to 1974-79 values.

The salient features which emerge from these data can be summarised as follows:

1. The reported prevalence of under-nutrition in children ('total' as well as 'severe') in all States was considerably less than those indicated by the NNMB reports. It seems unreasonable to assume that the difference in the prevalence of under-nutrition of the order observed can be totally accounted for by the fact that there was an interval of nearly five years between the latest NNMB report and the NFHS data. The difference may be attributable to the fact that the sampling designs were different, apart from the fact that NFHS operations covered far more States than what the NNMB had done. It would seem reasonable to argue that NNMB operations largely confined, as they were, to the

rural poor, captured relatively poorer and more deprived sections of the country's population than what the NFHS study did.

Table 16.3 : Ranking of States According to INSD

State	INSD Value	Rank
Kerala	0.741	1
Haryana	0.572	2
Tamil Nadu	0.558	3
Gujarat	0.552	4
Maharashtra	0.549	5
Karnataka	0.513	6
Andhra Pradesh	0.470	7
Assam	0.465	8
Orissa	0.456	9
Rajasthan	0.455	10
Madhya Pradesh	0.436	11
Uttar Pradesh	0.415	12

Index of Nutrition and Social Development.

Whatever may be the explanation, and irrespective of which of the two surveys is truly representative of the country, the NFHS data provide a less depressing picture of the State of child nutrition in the country than the NNMB data. The prevalence of overall under-nutrition ranged from 28 per cent in Manipur and Kerala to just over 50 per cent in Bihar – generally considered among the most backward from the point of view of health/nutrition; severe malnutrition likewise ranged from around 6 per cent in Kerala and Manipur to just over 25 per cent (again in Bihar).

2. Gender differences with respect to both total and severe under-nutrition appear even less remarkable than in the NNMB data, and the girl-child does not seem to be worse off than her counterpart in most States.

3. Neonatal mortality ranged from 15.5 per 1000 live birth in

Kerala to 54.8 in Bihar with Madhya Pradesh closely following with 53.2. Infant mortality rates also followed the same pattern with Bihar being the worst. Under-five mortality was 32 in Kerala as against 130 in Madhya Pradesh, Bihar and Orissa.

On the basis of all these data it would appear that Bihar, Madhya Pradesh and Orissa would rank among the most backward, and Kerala, Goa, Manipur, Nagaland and Mizoram among the best of the States surveyed.

4. There is generally a rough correspondence between performance with respect to child mortality and child nutrition in most States. States with the lowest child mortality rates have the lowest prevalence of child malnutrition (e.g. Kerala, Manipur, Nagaland, and Goa). While those with the worst performance with respect to child mortality (Orissa, Assam, Bihar and Uttar Pradesh and Madhya Pradesh and Rajasthan) being also the worst with respect to child nutrition.

In this connection, it may be mentioned that the NFHS data also provide a more favourable picture of demographic indicators such as the SRS (Sample Random Surveys). This would again raise the question of the relative representatives of the different samples.

SPECIFIC NUTRITIONAL PROBLEMS

Low Birth Weights (LBW)

Data from community studies show that a distressing level of over 30% of all infants born in India are of low birth weight (< 2.5 kg) reflecting maternal malnutrition and consequent intrauterine growth retardation. Recent advances in our knowledge indicate that low birth weights in full term babies carries not only serious short-term implications (e.g. increased neonatal mortality and growth failure) but also long-term implications in adults (e.g. increased susceptibility to diabetes and coronary heart disease in adult life).

The latest ICMR surveys compared to earlier studies show that there has been no significant improvement with respect to the incidence of low birth-weight deliveries; though there are some hospital-based data which suggest improvement.

It is important that the factors underlying the high incidence of LBW deliveries are identified and the problem effectively combated.

Iron Deficiency Anaemia

Perhaps the most widespread nutritional deficiency disease in the country is iron-deficiency anaemia, which though not spectacular in its manifestations contributes significantly towards impairment of functional efficiency, immunocompetence and learning ability. In women of the reproductive age group, it is a major factor contributing to maternal morbidity and mortality. It may also be an important factor responsible for the incidence of low-birth weight deliveries referred to above.

Extensive studies carried out under the auspices of the Indian Council of Medical Research had shown that the current strategy for combating anaemias of pregnancy through the distribution of iron-folate tablets to pregnant women in the last trimester of pregnancy has made a limited impact. It is clear that some additional inputs are necessary.

Iodine Deficiency Disorders

There has been an intensification of efforts to control goitre and iodine deficiency disorders in recent years. The earlier bottlenecks for production of adequate amounts of iodated salt have been cleared by the decision to end the State monopoly for the production of iodated salt. The earlier practice of providing subsidies to private manufacturers for the iodation of the salt has now been withdrawn. It is gratifying that despite this the overall production of iodised salt in the country does not seem to have suffered. Even so, logistic problems with respect to several important components in the chain of operations involved in goitre control have not been totally eliminated. The problems of ensuring quality-control of the iodation process and of ensuing adequate levels of iodine at the level of actual consumption are still formidable and have not been fully solved. In the meanwhile, the emergence of new areas of goitre – endemicity has introduced a new dimension. The reasons for such emergence are not clear. Whether soil iodine depletion consequent on modern agricultural technologies or whether new goitrogens – natural and commercial – are involved remains to be satisfactorily elucidated.

Other Micro-Nutrient Deficiencies

There has been a steep decline in the incidence of severe clinical form of vitamin A deficiency (Kerotamalacia) in recent years. The Statement that Kerotamalacia and vitamin A deficiency are a "major cause of blindness" in the country is just not true. We do see milder forms of Vitamin A deficiency. The strategy of promoting administration of massive doses of synthetic Vitamin A, as a prophylactic measure was introduced in India over 25 years ago when Keratomalacia was a major public health problem which it is not at present. It is unwise and unnecessary to continue to depend on this approach as mainstay for the control of Vitamin A deficiency in our mothers and children. The problem of vitamin A deficiency can and must be successfully combated and controlled through the judicious use of carotene-rich foods abundantly available in the country.

The logical approach for combating vitamin A deficiency is to promote the consumption of green leafy vegetables and other carotene rich foods by mothers in the last trimester of pregnancy, when there is significant transfer of maternal vitamin A to the foetus. Improvement of maternal diets through the inclusion of carotene-rich foods will contribute only to the betterment of the vitamin A nutritional status of the mother but also to improve hepatic stores of vitamin A in the infant; and possibly also towards augmentation of vitamin A concentration of breast milk of the mother during lactation. The use of massive doses of synthetic vitamin A in pregnancy is clearly prohibited because of the known teratogenic effects of such use.

Fortunately, India is blessed with a large array of carotene rich vegetables and fruits which can be put to judicious use for this purpose. At present, however, these foods do not figure prominently especially in the diets of pregnant women and infants. Special efforts are necessary to overcome this situation. A recent claim "based on a questionable study design, that the consumption of green leafy vegetables may not help to control the vitamin A deficiency, will not stand scientific scrutiny".

However, some practical steps will be necessary in order to promote the consumption of carotene-rich foods in the habitual Indian diets. There are wide varietal and locational differences with respect to carotene content are carotenoid profiles of these foods, as also with respect to their content of other nutrients. It is important to identify varieties of good nutritive value and culinary properties and acceptability and selectively propagate them. This was done in the case of wheat and rice with great success. Seeds of such good varieties must be widely distributed in order to promote home gardens. Also there is a need to identify appropriate culinary practices which will improve the acceptability of GLVs and will help in retaining their nutritive value. Considerable research is called for in these areas, which are currently neglected. There is also a need to identify strategies for large-scale production of carotene-rich foods, and especially of green leafy vegetables (GLVs) and for developing appropriate village-based techniques for their dehydration and storage for the avoidance of wastage and for use in lean seasons, and for use in large-scale supplementary feeding programmes – such as those of the ICDS and school meal programmes. In these later programmes, the inclusion of GLVs must be made mandatory. Innovative ways of making this feasible will have to be worked out.

It is not often realised that the incidence of vitamin B complex deficiencies in our mothers and children in our country is much higher than that of vitamin A deficiency. Recent multicentric studies of ICMR have clearly shown this. It is strange that international groups "who are very active" with respect to vitamin A deficiency are silent with respect to vitamin B complex deficiency.

The important message that emerges from the fact of the

presence of multiple deficiencies in our poor income groups, is that the answer with respect to their intervention does not lie in the pharmaceutical (drug-based) approach of distributing a few vitamins (singly or in combination) but in bringing about overall dietary improvement. Recent studies have in fact shown that foods (especially plant foods) contain besides nutrients, a wide array of bioactive phytochemicals, such as antioxidant blocking agents etc. that play important role in the prevention and control of "non-nutritional" diseases. It will be difficult to devise a pill or a tablet which can mimic the protective and preventive actions of natural foods.

EMERGING CHALLENGES

Recent developments point to the emergence of new dimensions to the food/nutrition problems.

Urbanisation

The ongoing migration of rural populations to urban areas (the urban population in India may well exceed 300 million by the turn of the century) introduces new dimensions. Urbanisation involves social changes in family structure, in living styles, in occupational pattern and dietary practices. These challenges must be addressed.

Expansion of Affluent Middle Class

With the progressive expansion of the ranks of the middle class, there has been a progressive increase in the incidence of diseases related to malnutrition (as opposed to undernutrition among the poor). The problem of obesity and of degenerative diseases are gathering disturbing dimensions with the result that the country may have to carry a double burden of problems of overnutrition at one end of the economic spectrum and problems of undernutrition of the poor at the other end.

Commercial Exploitation of Malnutrition

With increasing awareness of the importance of nutrition, increasing attempts at commercial exploitation of malnutrition by commercial interests – both national and international – must be expected. Some of the false international leads designed to promote drug based (as opposed to food-based approach) to the solution of our nutrition problems are examples of such attempts at commercial exploitation. Within the country itself, the mushrooming of a large number of slimming joints promising rapid weight reduction regimes using hush-hush slimming and dieting procedures are yet another example of commercial exploitation. These aberrations are likely to gather further momentum in the years to come and will need to be combated effectively.

Thus, as we move into the next millennium formidable challenges and opportunities with respect to improvement of the nutritional status of our population will unfold. It is to be hoped that we would be able to summon the wisdom to use these opportunities and to respond to these challenges.

ANNEXURE I

State-wise Comparison of Nutritional Status and Mortality Rates of Children under 4 years.
(NFHS DATA - 1992-93)

State	Sex of child	Nutritional Status (wt-for-age)		Mortality Rates (Boys & Girls pooled)			
		<–3SD	<–2SD	Neo natal	Infant (0.1)	Child (4.1)	Under 5 (5.0)
Andhra Pradesh	M	13.8	47.1	45.3	70.4	22.4	91.2
	F	17.5	51.1				
Arunachal Pradesh	M	12.8	35.2	17.5	40.0	33.3	72.0
	F	15.0	36.6				
Assam	M	19.4	52.4	50.9	88.7	58.7	142.2
	F	18.01	48.5				
Bihar	M	25.7	55.5	54.8	89.2	42.0	127.5
	F	24.7	48.5				
Delhi	M	12.7	41.6	34.9	65.4	19.0	83.1
	F	11.3	41.6				
Goa	M	8.7	35.6	20.6	31.9	7.2	38.9
	F	9.0	34.0				
Gujarat	M	15.0	41.6	42.3	68.7	37.9	104.0
	F	14.9	46.7				
Haryana	M	7.5	34.9	38.4	73.3	27.4	98.7
	F	10.8	41.6				
Himachal Pradesh	M	11.2	34.2	55.8	41.1	69.1	—
	F	6.9	28.3				
Karnataka	M	18.4	52.9	45.3	65.4	23.5	87.3
	F	20.5	55.8				
Kerala	M	5.4	28.8	15.5	23.8	8.4	32.0
	F	6.9	28.3				
Madhya Pradesh	M	17.6	53.0	53.2	65.2	49.3	130.3
	F	20.4	49.1				
Maharashtra	M	18.5	51.3	36.4	50.5	20.9	70.3
	F	22.0	54.0				
Manipur	M	7.1+	28.1	25.1	42.4	30.2	61.7
	F	6.0	27.6				
Meghalaya	M	18.0	49.2	37.8	64.2	24.3	86.9
	F	15.8	41.2				
Mizoram	M	5.5	26.9	8.3	14.6	14.9	29.3
	F	5.2	29.5				
Nagaland	M	7.8	30.4	10.0	17.2	3.6	20.7
	F	7.1	24.8				

(Contd.)

State	Sex of child	Nutritional Status (wt-for-age)			Mortality Rates (Boys & Girls pooled)		
		<–3SD	<–2SD	Neo natal	Infant (0.1)	Child (4.1)	Under 5 (5.0)
Orissa	M	22.0	53.4	64.7	112.1	21.3	131.0
	F	23.6	53.2				
Rajasthan	M	18.4	42.5	37.2	72.6	32.3	—
	F	20.2	40.5				
Tamil Nadu	M	11.5	43.1	46.2	67.7	20.1	86.5
	F	13.8	49.7				
Tripura	M	15.5	46.5	43.6	75.8	31.2	104.6
	F	19.9	49.3				
Uttar Pradesh	M	19.3	51.8	59.9	99.9	46.0	141.3
	F	19.2	47.8				
West Bengal	M	16.4	52.9	51.8	75.3	26.0	99.3
	F	18.3	56.6				

F=Female
M=Male

APPENDICES

APPENDIX–1

WORLD FOOD PROBLEMS : THE MAIN ISSUE IN 1982

FOREWORD

This booklet contains two papers. The first discusses the most pressing world food issues and the remedial measures requiring urgent attention during 1982. The second describes the overall nature of world food problems. It illustrates their complexity and outlines the long-term technical and political action required to resolve them.

It is easy, at the present time, to be pessimistic about the chances of achieving effective international action to end world hunger. The effects of recession are being increasingly felt in industrialised countries which are the major donors of material and technical resources for world food and agricultural development. There is a real possibility that concern with domestic problems and will tend to reduce earlier widespread support for international action to assist poorer nations and people.

It is particularly significant that despite some progress made towards world food security during the 1970s, the situation remains dangerously fragile and, with diminished will to continue necessary support, it could deteriorate rapidly. Increasing interdependence in our modern world means that all countries and people, rich and poor alike, must help to solve food issues.

The major issue for World Food Day in 1982 may well be how to revive the interest of the peoples and governments of the industrialized countries in helping to eliminate hunger, malnutrition and poverty. The efforts and sacrifices of the past are in danger of being wasted as a result of myopia or misunderstanding of what has been achieved and of what is possible.

Background Paper circulated by FAO for the World Food Day, 1982.

The solution of world food problems depends above all on the elimination of poverty by means of increasingly self-reliant action in the developing countries. The industrialized countries, however, have a very important role as well.

The summit meeting on cooperation and development, held at Canoun, Mexico, in October 1981, gave considerable emphasis to food problems. It also clearly stated the need for a joint effort between rich and poor countries.

"Sustained and long-term international efforts as well as internal efforts on the part of the developing countries to attain increasing self-sufficiency in food production is the basic element in obtaining a real answer to the problems of hunger. Nevertheless, this effort requires timely and sufficient international technical and financial support in co-ordination with international policies and strategies."[1]

Such impressive statements have not been rare in the past. There has long been inter-governmental agreement on a wide range of objectives and even specific targets for overcoming world food problems. But the record of their implementation is dismal, and is in danger of becoming even worse.

Not only the struggle to overcome food problems but the whole international development effort is jeopardized by a probable stagnation in foreign assistance. The reduction in the resources of the World Bank's soft-loan affiliate, the International Development Association (IDA), is especially serious, since it has been the biggest source of assistance for food and agriculture in the poorest developing countries. Official development assistance for agriculture already fell in "real" terms, allowing for inflation, in 1979 and recovered only partially in 1980, the latest year for which there are full data.[2] In the face of pressing domestic problems, many industrialized countries are also turning back to greater nationalism and protectionism in their trade policies.

Especially since the United Nations World Food Conference was held in 1974, the international consensus on how to attack world food problems has been progressively refined and improved. More and more developing countries are also recognising the need to give much higher priority to food and agricultural development and have adopted improved policies. Some of them have already accomplished a great deal with very limited resources. It would be particularly unfortunate if the action of some of the major industrialized countries in support of their efforts should begin to flag at this time.

A main issue in 1982 is, therefore, to try to revive the interest of the people and governments of the industrialized countries in helping to eliminate hunger and malnutrition. As is discussed below, action is mainly needed in the form of increased development assistance for food and agriculture, a higher guaranteed level of food aid, adequate reserve stocks of food, and international trade measures in favour of developing countries. All of this action should be directed above all to the poorest countries in the world community and to the poorest people in these countries.

Reviving the interest of the industrialized countries in solving world food problems is no easy task. The general political and economic climate is probably less propitious for development assistance and for concessions to developing countries than at any time since the establishment of the United Nations system in the idealistic aftermath of the second world war.

Political and Economic Climate

Very little progress has been made in implementing the Declaration and Programme of Action on the Establishment of a New International Economic Order adopted by the Sixth Special Session of the United Nations General Assembly as long ago as 1974. In spite of recent initiatives like the report of the Brandt Commission[3] in 1980 and the Cancun Summit in 1981, there is still no effective North-South dialogue.

The industrialized countries are preoccupied with serious problems of recession, unemployment, inflation, currency instability and energy supplies. Such problems are even worse in most developing countries and are seriously affecting their poorer people. However, the industrialized countries are increasingly turning inward in their search for solutions. Some of them have their own costly food and agricultural problems. Some, in contrast to their policies in the depression years of the 1930s, are even reducing social welfare expenditures for the poorer groups in their own populations. They believe that they have little to spare at present for assistance to poor people in the rest of the world.

Multilateral assistance is particularly under attack, and some important donor governments prefer to provide development assistance bilaterally rather than through multilateral organisations which they regard as inefficient and over which they have little direct control. There is a new insistence on economic efficiency and productivity and on a greater role for the private sector. Priority for food and agriculture may need to be reaffirmed in relation to newer pre-occupations like energy supplies. The assessments made by international organizations of the incidence of poverty and hunger are also sometimes questioned.

Some of these attitudes can easily be deplored. Since they exist, however, they must be faced realistically if progress is to be achieved in overcoming world food problems.

Priority for Food and Agriculture

Following an earlier phase of overemphasis on rapid industrialization, it has for some time been recognized that high priority should be given to food and agriculture in most developing countries. It is sometimes suggested that the case for this priority (in competition, for example, with energy), in national development programmes and in development assistance, now needs to be reassessed in the light of the changed conditions of the 1980s.

Adequate food nevertheless remains the most basic of all human needs. The food and agricultural sector still provides the basis for a large part of the industrial production and export earnings of most of the developing countries without oil resources. The need to create employment and income-earning opportunities for the rural poor through increased food and agricultural production remains an over-riding consideration. If the sector required a large share of the available resources before, it is surely logical that it should receive an ever larger share at a time of diminishing resources.

Many developing countries are now giving higher priority to food and agriculture than in the past. There are numerous examples of new and more concrete national food and nutrition strategies, policies, plans or programmes, usually prepared with international assistance. This encouraging trend could be reinforced by further assistance, not just for their preparation but also for the action required to implement them.

Success Stories

The statistics of world poverty and hunger provided by the international community are sometimes branded as exaggerating the magnitude of the problems still to be overcome. FAO's estimate of more than 400 million seriously undernourished people in the mid-1970s is a favourite target for such criticism. Although there are much lower estimates, there are others too that are much higher. FAO has always emphasised that the figure could be no more than a very rough approximation, in view of the limited knowledge of the availability and particularly the distribution of food supplies, and of the differing nutritional requirements of individual people.

Controversy over this figure is not very fruitful. Whatever the correct one may be, even the lower estimates indicate a shamefully large number of undernourished people in the world. The figure is not used in an operational sense as the basis for targets and programmes. Estimates of requirements in such areas as increased food production in developing countries, investment, financial assistance, food aid and stock levels are based mainly on the generally much surer data of food production and trade.

It is true, however, that in calling for more assistance for developing countries the international community has usually placed the main emphasis on the gravity of the problems still to be overcome. This is natural and certainly not intended to exaggerate. But it may have tended to conceal the progress, however, limited, that has already been made and the successes that have been achieved. It has thus probably contributed in no small measure to the present disillusionment with development assistance in a number of industrialized countries.

It is, therefore, desirable to pay greater attention to publicising past successes, many of which are partly attributable to international assistance. The resolution of the Twentieth Session of the FAO Conference in 1979 that instituted World Food Day emphasized the need "to draw attention to successes achieved in food and agricultural development."[4]

In some cases it is simply a question of showing the other side of the coin. For instance, FAO estimates that the number of seriously undernourished people in the developing market economies[5] rose by about 75 million in the first half of the 1970s. The same figures also suggest that it was possible to nourish fairly adequately more than two-thirds of the 230 million increase in the population of these countries during this period, but this achievement is rarely mentioned. Similarly it is often stated that in more than half of the developing countries food production did not keep up with population growth in the 1970s. This also means that it succeeded in doing so in about half of them. These more successful ones have well over half the total population of the developing countries.

The expansion of food and agricultural production in the 1970s in the developing countries as a whole failed by a wide margin to reach the target of an average of 4 per cent a year set in the International Development Strategy (IDS) for the Second United Nations Development Decade (DD2). This target was an ambitious one in comparison with past trends. Although they were insufficient, the increases actually achieved (3.2 per cent a year in food production and 3.1 per cent in total agricultural production) thus still represent a remarkable performance.

A number of individual developing countries have recently made notable, if sometimes temporary, progress towards greater self-sufficiency in basic foods. These include India (cereals) and Bangladesh, Indonesia and the Philippines (rice). They were formerly large recipients of development assistance but have been able to become less dependent on it.

Internationally supported cereal breeding programmes have had a tremendous impact on food production in these and many other developing countries. This success story has, however, tended to be obscured by the emphasis placed in some undesirable socio-economic effects of the accompanying "green revolution". It is certainly urgently necessary to evolve less costly and more self-reliant technologies that are more suitable for poor, small-scale farmers. It is also essential to make structural changes to ensure a more equitable distribution of the benefits of technological progress, as it is clearly brought out in the Declaration and Programme of Action adopted by the World Conference on Agrarian Reform and Rural Development (WCARRD) in 1979.[6] But the boost given by the green revolution technology to food production in many parts of the undernourished, developing world, cannot be denied.

World Food Security

Progress in the broad area of world food security offers a good example of the mixture of successes and failures that has been experienced. In its widest sense, world food security encompasses both the need for greater food self-sufficiency in developing countries already discussed (including the need for most of the production increases to come from their poor, small farmers) and the need for improved conditions in world trade that is discussed later. In a narrower sense it is particularly concerned with the access of poor countries to adequate food supplies in times of shortage, and thus with food aid and reserve stocks.

An important early step in improving world food security was the establishment in FAO in 1975 of the Global Information and Early Warning System on Food and Agriculture. This is a good example of the kind of work that can only be done multilaterally. Often based on confidential information, it helps both individual countries and the international community to be prepared in advance to meet food emergencies.

A recent step forward was the establishment in May 1981 of a "Food Facility" by the International Monetary Fund (IMF). This extends its Compensatory Financing Facility to give credit to countries with balance of payments problems resulting from exceptionally high cereal import bills.

Also in 1981 the target of 500,000 tons of cereals a year for the International Emergency Food Reserve (IEFR) was reached at last for the first time since it was set by the Seventh Special Session of the General Assembly in 1975. On the other hand, the target of an annual minimum of 10 million tons of food aid in cereals, agreed as long ago as 1974 at the World Food Conference, has never yet quite been met. Such aid has been falling since the 1979-80 crop season. This is mainly because most food aid commitments are still made in financial rather than physical terms. Food aid thus tends to drop when world supplies are shorter and prices higher – the very circumstances in which it is most needed.

Both these targets must now be regarded as outdated and inadequate. While food aid has been much lower in recent years than the peak levels of the 1950s and 1960s, the food import requirements of the developing countries have in the meantime increased enormously. In 1981-82 food aid is expected to cover only 18 per cent of the food import requirements of the "food aid priority countries"[7], as against 28 per cent as recently as 1976-77. FAO, therefore, estimates that food aid in cereals should rise to 17 to 18.5 million tons a year by the mid–1980s if the poorer developing countries are to be able to obtain the food imports they need. A floor level of at least 10 million tons a year should be formally guaranteed in physical terms by a new Food Aid Convention (FAC).

Food emergencies, especially those involving large numbers of refugees, have become very frequent. The target for the IEFR should therefore be progressively increased, possibly to as much as 2 million tons by 1985. Voluntary undertakings should assure contributions for two or three years ahead, as well as their availability for multilateral use through the United Nations/FAO World Food Programme (WFP). The WFP has had to use an increasing proportion of its resources for emergencies, to the detriment of its work for development. By the end of 1981 pledges to it for the 1981-82 biennium were only US$769 million, as against the target of $ 1,000 million.

The key element in an effective system of world food security is still conspicuously missing. This is an internationally coordinated series of national reserve stocks, held by both developed and developing countries. Ideally they would be coordinated through a new International Grains Arrangement or Wheat Trade Convention, with legally binding provisions on both prices and stocks, aimed at minimising price fluctuations in world markets and ensuring the availability of supplies, especially for poor countries, when and where needed. While an international agreement of this nature must remain a major goal, it is clear from the protracted negotiations of the last few years that there is little change of attaining it in the near future. In the meantime, every effort should be made to establish more effectively voluntary arrangements.

The opportunity to establish a viable system of reserve stocks was missed when the record level of total cereal stocks made it easier a few years ago. These stocks are now rising again. Every year that the setting up of the necessary reserves is delayed, their costs will increase, because of population growth as well as price inflation. Interest rates have also increased.

Many developing countries vulnerable to food shortages require additional food aid and financial and technical assistance to establish food security stocks. A large number of them now have specific food stock policies. While some collective arrangements have taken shape, many individual countries do not have the resources to implement these policies. FAO estimates that domestic and external investment in the storage and other facilities required for food security in developing countries needs to rise to US$ 1,000 million a year in real terms for at least a decade.

While some progress has been achieved in world food security (particularly in comparison with the dangerous situation in the early 1970s), it is still very fragile. More progress has been made in increasing the capability of the international community for meeting short-term emergencies than in the longer-term aspects of world food security, such as accelerating the increase in food production in developing countries and building a permanent system of reserve stocks. The action already taken to achieve world food security has been substantial, although it has never been sufficient and there are crucial missing elements. Enough progress has been made, however, for it to be foolish not press on and consolidate it as quickly as possible.

Africa and the Poorest Countries

Nowhere in the world is food security as fragile as in the poorest countries, as especially in Africa, where so many of them are found. Crop failures have been very frequent in Africa recently, and there has been an alarming deterioration in food self-sufficiency. Food production per head of the population has dropped by more than 10 per cent in the past decade, an average dietary energy supplies have been barely maintained at 6 to 7 per cent below nutritional requirements. Food imports have more than doubled in volume and risen five times in cost. In many countries there has recently been a reversal of the trend towards a reduction in infant mortality, much of which is caused directly or indirectly by inadequate food.

The preparation by FAO of a Regional Food Plan for Africa[8] constituted an important first step in identifying and quantifying the measures required to redress this disturbing situation. This was followed by the adoption by the Organisation of African Unity in April 1980 of the Lagos Plan of Action, which gives high priority to food and agriculture.

A much higher proportion of food aid and financial and technical assistance has to be directed to the poorest countries that are most in need of it. It is, therefore, encouraging that the share of the least-developed countries[9] in total development assistance for agriculture increased in 1980. Donors undertook to give priority to these countries at the United Nations Conference on the Least Developed Countries in September 1981.

Agricultural Investment

FAO's study of *Agriculture: Toward 2000*[10] shows on a global scale what could be accomplished in solving world food and agricultural problems if there were a sufficient expansion in the national and international effort. The main requirement, as stressed already, is a rapid acceleration of the increase in the food and agricultural production of the developing countries, most of which should come from their poor, small-scale farmers.

This will entail a massive increase in agricultural investment in these countries, particularly for land and water development. While most of this must be generated by the developing countries themselves, increased development assistance is an essential component because of the difficult balance of payments situation of most of those without oil resources. Assistance requirements are estimated (in 1975 prices) to rise to some $15 to 18 billion a year by 2000, of which about 80 per cent for investment and the rest for current inputs and technical assistance. Help in obtaining essential supplies of fertilizers and other inputs is particularly important. Technical assistance requirements also remain large, especially for training and institution building. It is, however, necessary to be more sensitive to the fact that (in some degree as a result of international training programme) the nature of the need is changing in most countries towards much more specialized and higher-level foreign experts than were required in the past.

The increase in development assistance that is needed in large only in relation to past levels (less than $ 5 billion a year in 1980 at 1975 prices). It is common place to observe that it is completely dwarfed by armaments expenditures, but it is even small in relation to such items of personal consumption expenditure as tobacco products and alcoholic beverages in the United States or in the EEC.

It is often claimed that the developing countries have a limited absorptive capacity for further assistance. This is certainly true in some cases, especially in the least-developed countries, although it could frequently be remedied by more assistance in project preparation. In Africa alone FAO has identified additional technical assistance requirements valued at about $ 650 million. Absorptive capacity could also be increased if donors (including some of the international agencies) would simplify their procedures and, particularly for the poorest countries, finance a larger proportion of local currency costs.

Trade Questions

The developing countries' need for developing assistance would be reduced if they could obtain wider markets and higher prices for their exports. Agricultural products are still the source of about a third of the export earnings of the developing countries without oil resources. Agricultural exports are particularly important for those countries that import staple foods in return for them.

Larger export earnings for both agricultural and (increasingly) non-agricultural products would greatly help developing countries to finance not only essential food imports, but also the import of the capital and other goods such as fertilizers required for their food and agricultural development. Trade is, therefore, a key aspect of world food problems.

Recent trends in world commodity prices have generally not favoured the developing countries, and continued fluctuations have hampered their development planning. A main need is for more stable prices at levels offering a fair reward to producers. The entry into Operation of the Common Fund for Commodities would be an important step towards this, but is still awaits ratification by a sufficient number of countries. The fund is designed to help finance buffer stocks and commodity development programmes. The "STABEX" scheme of the European Economic Community (EEC) has helped to stabilize the export earnings of a limited number of countries, and it is desirable that this and further such schemes should be extended as soon as possible to cover all low-income countries.

A second main need is for the reduction of removal of tariff and non-tariff barriers to imports into industrialized countries, especially of processed and semi-processed products – Some progress in tariff reduction has been made through the Generalized System of Preferences (GSP) and the successive rounds of Multilateral Trade Negotiations (MTN) under the General Agreement on Tariffs and Trade (GATT). Both require further extension to agricultural products of interests to developing countries. The forthcoming Ministerial Meeting of GATT provides a good opportunity for a new emphasis on agricultural products and the trade problems of low-income countries, including non-tariff barriers. There is the danger that protectionism will become even more prevalent in some industrialized countries if they continue to react to their economic difficulties by inward-looking policies.

Multilateral Assistance

Idealistic reasons no longer appear sufficient to guarantee public support for multilateral as against bilateral development assistance. A new, more practical case has to be made. Most of the arguments for such assistance are from the point of view of the recipient countries. In particular, multilateral assistance is not tied to purchases from donor countries, and its continuity is not at the mercy of political fluctuations. There are, however, other arguments that should appeal to donors as well.

Some of the major initiatives that are required concern problems common to many developing countries (such as basic agricultural research) on cross national boundaries (such as river basin development, the eradication and control of human and animal diseases, and marine fishery development). In some specialized fields (like the prevention of food losses) a multilateral programme can more easily assemble the necessary expertise and other basic resources needed for effective action. Many donor countries, particularly some of the smaller ones, prefer not to have to set up their own organisations for the preparation, appraisal and evaluation of development projects, but to work through the machinery already available in international institutions.

In 1980 about a third of the total multilateral development assistance was for agriculture, whereas the bilateral figure was only about 10 per cent. Multilateral agencies such as the World Bank and the International Fund for Agricultural Development (IFAD) have pioneered assistance for development projects aimed at the rural poor. The WFP has been able to adopt experimental approaches to the use of food aid for development and to provide emergency aid in politically sensitive situations.

The multilateral agencies also perform other functions in addition to development assistance. They provide essential objective information and analysis, and a forum where governments can meet to decide on international action.

At the same time, it is necessary for the multilateral agencies to respond to the call for a more hard-headed and efficient approach to development assistance. FAO has in fact already done this through its recent measures to prune its headquarters bureaucracy and concentrate more on direct action in the field.

Private Enterprise

Most of the world's food is produced by private farmers and their families who require incentives to enable and encourage them to produce more. They receive a wide range of government support in the industrialized countries, many of which have substantial government programmes and have stimulated a more rapid growth of production. The millions of poor small farmers in the developing world are even more in need of such public sector programmes to support them. President Reagan of the United States in his message on World Food Day 1981 noted that "many nations lack... the system of incentives to private enterprise that are critical to successful agriculture". Such programmes in developing countries often require international public development assistance to ensure their full effectiveness.

Furthermore, to ensure that incentives do actually enable farmers to raise crop and livestock yields and increase their own productivity, there must be complementary services and inputs which the private sector is not well placed to provide, especially in developing countries. These include the financing and organization of such things as research, extension and training services and the construction of rural roads and irrigation facilities.

Private enterprise – in the form of small local enterprises and large national or transnational corporations – plays a major role in the increasing and distribution of food. As developing countries move increasingly from subsistence to market agriculture, processing and distribution activities would expand. To ensure that private enterprise performs these functions efficiently and contributes to equitable development poses a major challenge.

The role of the private sector in agricultural development thus presents complex issues. The recommendations in the WCARRD Programme of Action provide a realistic and valuable guide in this regard.

World Solidarity

The preceding pages have indicated many areas of both trade and aid where enhanced efforts by industrialized countries (both market and centrally-planned economies[11]) are essential to help in overcoming world food problems. Much has already been achieved, but with a little more effort real progress could be in sight.

Food problems, even though mainly concentrated in one part of the world, are truly world problems. From the moral point of view this is more than obvious. Even from a less idealistic point of view, it must be recognized that inadequate supplies of food and other basic necessities of life lead to stresses between "have" and "have-not" countries and groups of people within countries. Such conflicts can be a principal cause of political instability. Adequate food for all provides much greater security and much better chance of world peace than vast expenditures on regularly outdated armaments.

Another important aspect of world solidarity lies in the collective responsibility for the precious natural resources on which food and agricultural production depends. In this regard the FAO Conference in 1981 adopted the World Soil Charter[12], containing a set of Principles and Guidelines for Action concerning wise land use. It also requested FAO to prepare the elements of a draft international convention for plant genetic resources.

The efforts asked far from the industrialized countries to help overcome world food problems are admittedly large, but they are minute in comparison with their own large resources and their equally large calls on the resources of the world as a whole. While they are at present suffering from serious economic and social ills, even their unemployed still enjoy levels of living far greater than most people in developing countries. Their protectionist measures, while at least temporarily preserving some jobs, even hurt their own consumers (through higher prices) as well as the developing countries. Food shortages in other parts of the world can damage them too by raising prices. Finally, their emergence from the present economic recession will be assisted greatly by prosperous, expanding markets for their exports in developing countries. These markets cannot be strong and prosperous, however, if the large food and agricultural sectors receive too little development assistance. With continued (although slower) population growth and gradual increases in incomes per head, demand in developing countries is likely to be a principal engine of economic growth, especially for world trade, in the long-term future.

The First World Food Day in 1981 was a remarkable demonstration of the solidarity concerning world food problems that exists between the people of all the world's many and diverse countries. Governments too were very fully involved. But while most governments fairly readily agree to what is needed, they are usually slow in taking the necessary action and especially in financing it.

A massive educational effort is still required to create greater awareness of the nature and gravity of world food problems, and to mobilize public opinion in favour of the types of action outlined here. The governments of some industrialized countries believe that they are actually ahead of public opinion in their own countries on development assistance policies. Many voluntary, non-governmental organisations are doing an important job of development education, but their work has not yet made sufficient impact on public opinion in general.

There is also an urban bias to public opinion in many developing countries, even these suffering from food shortages. The Director General of FAO has therefore urged the governments of developing countries to involve as far as possible in World Food Day activities the leaders of organizations of rural people. He has also indicated his readiness to seek, in the context of World Food Day, ways of assisting them in introducing food and nutritional subjects in school curricula. This would increase understanding not only of personal nutrition, but also of the place of food and agriculture in the national economy, and of world food problems in general.

It is to be hoped that in 1982 and subsequent years World Food Day can contribute to more positive action by governments. In developing countries this means action in favour of their poorest people, and in industrialized countries action in favour of the poorest countries in the world community.

THE OVERALL NATURE OF FOOD PROBLEMS

A few years ago, people were asked in a global survey if there had been times during the previous year when they did not have enough money to buy food. A significant proportion of people said "yes": over 70 per cent of those questioned in Africa south of the Sahara, 65 per cent in India, 42 per cent in Mexico, 15 per cent in Italy and 14 per cent in Japan and the United States.[13]

Ensuring that people do have access to sufficient food has long been a problem of concern to the international community. An extended series of meetings, including the World Food Congresses in 1963 and 1970, the 1974 Rome World Food Conference and the 1979 World Conference on Agrarian Reform and Rural Development (WCARRD), have defined and discussed the crisis and issued numerous policy statements. The Food and Agriculture Organisation of the United Nations works to achieve inter-governmental agreement on the proposed measures and promotes their implementation.

All too often, policies for which Governments have voted have not been implemented to realize the impact desired. Frequent calls have been made for the achievement of such goals as the elimination of severe undernutrition in the quickest possible time. That goal is achievable: the world has the money, the resources and the technology to reach it. However, it lacks the political commitment to channel the necessary resources toward development and towards the struggle to end hunger.

In order to strengthen that commitment, the FAO Conference of 1979 established World Food Day on 16 October each year, beginning in 1981. The Conference Resolution establishing World Food Day states its first objective as being to "heighten public awareness of the nature and dimensions of the long-term world food problem, and to develop further the sense of national and international solidarity in the struggle against hunger, malnutrition and poverty". Another was to "draw attention to successes achieved in food and agricultural development, as well as to emergency and other serious needs."[14]

World Food Day provides a new opportunity for the work of

FAO to become better known and understood. World Food Day also provides a channel for ideas and information on the ways in which food problems concern the ordinary person to become better known to the international community.

Effective action against hunger depends upon a thorough under-standing of the problem and the merits of proposed solutions. World Food Day also brings into relief the issues of why hunger exists and what must be done about it.

October 16 was selected as World Food Day since it is the anniversary of the founding of FAO on 16 October, 1945.

Nature and Dimensions of World Food Problems

Despite all the inter-governmental discussions and agreements since the acute food crisis of the early 1970s, the world still lacks a workable world food security system. Scanty food supplies in the developing countries remain vulnerable to the effects of droughts, floods and other disasters. Over 9 million refugees crowd many developing nations, stretching meagre supplies even thinner. Meanwhile chronic hunger and malnutrition persist even in years of good harvest.

FAO estimates that the number of severely undernourished people in the developing market economies[15] rose from about 360 million in 1969–71 to about 435 million (23 per cent of the population of these countries) in 1974–76.[16] Other estimates are even higher.

Appallingly large numbers of people suffer debilitating ill health because they do not have enough to eat. A disproportionate number of them are young children. Poor nutrition contributes, indirectly as well as directly, to the high rates of infant mortality still found in the developing countries.

Inadequate diets have many implications. For example, people can suffer protein deficiencies even if they have enough protein in their diets. If they are not eating enough calories to provide their bodies with energy, some of the protein they eat will be used for that purpose.

A diet without necessary nutrients leads to crippling illnesses. Lack of vitamin A causes blindness. Insufficient iodine leads to goitre. Without the iron they need, women become anemic.

Wherever it exists, poverty is the prime cause of hunger. Without enough land to grow food, or enough money to buy it, people will be hungry. Harvest short-falls cause price increases that hit the poor the hardest because they spend such a large proportion of their meagre income in food.

Even in richer, industrialized countries, poverty can mean hunger. Many people there – especially the aged, racial minorities, and families headed by women – suffer from serious nutritional deficiencies. For others in the richer nations, affluence brings different nutritional problems, through the many serious diseases that are connected with overeating the many serious diseases that are connected with overeating and obesity.

Food Production and Distribution

Solving current food problems depends on two main factors: very rapid increases in food production and more equitable access to food supplies.

World supplies of dietary energy are now about 10 per cent more than the nutritional requirements of the population. Even the supplies available in the developing countries would be nearly sufficient to meet domestic needs, if they were distributed strictly in accordance with these requirements. In fact, to a large extent, levels of income determine how food is distributed among the population. Thus some people (particularly in industrialized countries) consume more than their nutritional requirements, and many people (especially in developing countries) consume less.

Available food supplies can be redistributed through such measures as food aid, supplementary feeding programmes, selective subsidies, and low prices shops. Redistribution of food sufficient to eliminate hunger and malnutrition, however, would entail massive reapportionment both among and within countries – not necessarily a feasible undertaking. The only solution is the redistribution of income and the reduction of poverty.

The amounts of food produced must be increased, and dramatically. A 4 per cent target for average yearly increase in the developing countries' food and agricultural production has been called for often: in 1970, in the International Development Strategy for the Second United Nations Development Decade; in 1974, by the World Food Conference; in 1980, by the International Strategy for the Third Development Decade.

That goal remains unrealized. During the 1970s the actual rate of increase was little more than 3 per cent a year. In more than half the developing nations, production did not keep up with population growth, let alone with the increased demand for food resulting from people (usually in towns) earning higher incomes. In general, production increases were smallest where they were most needed – in the poorest countries.

In fact, in some parts of the world food production per capita has fallen. Today, the average African has 10 per cent less to eat than a decade ago.

Finally, most production increases have come from larger farmers. This results in part from the introduction of "green revolution" agriculture, which works only for those who can afford the costly technology it requires: improved seeds, chemical fertilizers and pesticides, water control. Small farmers, who must play a central role in effort to overcome their own hunger, as well as that of others, have often been bypassed by agricultural development during the past decades.

The negative aspects of recent history receive the most attention. As the resolution establishing World Food Day implies, however, the "successes achieved" also deserve notice. India, for example, has recently achieved self-sufficiency in cereals. The Philippines have eliminated their rice deficit.

The future must bring many more successes, with the developing countries increasing their food production much faster than in the past.

By building up their agricultural self-reliance, they can lessen their dependence on increasingly expensive food imports. While the volume of cereals imported by the most seriously affected developing nations and least developed nations increased by 14 per cent between 1967–69 and 1976–78, the prices they paid almost doubled and freight bills quadrupled.

Efforts to increase food production also make it possible to involve far more people in food production and planning processes. New jobs can be created in the rural sector, especially for women.

FAO's study *Agricultrue: Towards 2000* indicates that the needed production increases are possible. They will, however, require immense financing, dwarfing past efforts. *Agriculture: Toward 2000* projects 1990 external agricultural assistance needs at $ 11 to 12.5 billion.[17] Yet when this sum of money is compared with military expenditures it appears minuscule. The annual global military bill now totals about $ 550 billion.[18]

An Agenda for the Developing World

It will be difficult for the developing nations to expand their agricultural production as rapidly as they must.

Large investments will be needed to open up new land and to expand and improve irrigation, because most accessible land is already being farmed. While agricultural areas can still be extended without ecological damage in some parts of the world, most of the growth in production must come from higher yields on land already in use. Agriculture must make much more use of chemical and organic fertilizers, improved seeds, and pesticides. Mechanization must be encouraged judiciously, where it will raise production without unnecessarily creating unemployment.

While production expands, care must be taken for the environment, especially by conserving precious soil and water. Agriculture uses large quantities of scarce and expensive fossil fuel, notably for chemical fertilizers and farm machinery. Wherever possible in the food system, less energy should be used, above all in food processing and distribution in the industrialized countries. More widespread use should be made of organic fertilizers, now largely wasted. At the same time, availability of essential energy supplies to agriculture should be assured. Agricultural production uses only a moderate share – 3 to 4 per cent – of total world consumption of commercial energy.[19]

Whether or not increased agricultural production succeeds in lessening hunger and malnutrition depends to a very large extent on how it is done. Not only is people's participation in the institutions and systems which govern them a basic human right, according to WCARRD, but "Rural development strategies can realize their full potential only through the motivation, active involvement and organisation at the grass-roots level of rural people, with special emphasis on the least advantaged."[20] Many people who have until now been excluded – women in particular, landless labourers, small farmers and fishers generally – must become deeply involved in the work and in the direction of the development process.

Government agricultural services, including research, education, extension, marketing and credit, must be reoriented to meet the needs of small producers. In many countries, agrarian reform would enable the rural poor to have access to and control over land and other productive resources. People's organizations, through which rural people participate in development, should be encouraged and supported.

Finally, in view of the difficulties facing the developing countries as they try to increase food production so rapidly, it is essential to get as much as possible out of what can be produced.

Reducing huge but avoidable food losses can greatly expand the available supplies. In 1975 the Seventh Special Session of the United Nations General Assembly called for the reduction of post-harvest losses by at least half within a decade. In 1977 the FAO Conference established an Action Programme for the Prevention of Food Losses, which concentrates on basic food-stuffs in the farm and village. This can mean more food for the rural poor, by conserving supplies, including the large part that never enters the market. More efficient marketing and processing would also help resolve the dilemma of how to encourage producers without increasing prices too much. Nutrition education can assist consumers to eat better without spending more.

Economic Assistance - Mutual Aid

Most of the action required to eliminate hunger and malnutrition in the developing countries inevitably depends on the governments, the farmers and other rural people of these countries themselves. Their efforts, and international solidarity for them, constitute a main focus of World Food Day.

It is of critical importance to recognize the central role of agriculture, not only in the economies of the developing world, but internationally.

The economies of all the world's nations have become so interdependent that debility in one sector will weaken many others. The Brandt Report[21] rightly pinpoints numerous ways in which economic health in the nations of the South would benefit the North. For example, the widespread shortfalls in food supplies that are likely to occur if the developing nations do not dramatically increase production could bring on even more rampant inflation of food prices in the industrialized world.

Further, because human survival depends upon adequate food, and because access to that food is a human right, a world where so many are malnourished will be insecure and conflict ridden. Justice and peace cannot coexist with widespread hunger.

The Involvement of the Industrialized World

Industrialized countries should give direct support to the efforts made by developing countries, and indirect support through the creation of an improved structure of international relations. Many needed changes were proposed in the Declaration and Programme of Action on a New International Economic Order, adopted by the Sixth Special Session of the General Assembly in 1974. Unfortunately, progress toward implementation of these changes has been extremely slow.

While many developing countries have failed to meet their production targets, most industrialized countries have not reached agreed targets for resource flows. Only a few of the smaller industrialized countries have contributed 0.7 per cent of their GNP to official development assistance, meeting the long-standing international target.

A target for external assistance to food and agriculture was included in the Strategy and Guidelines for International

Agricultural Adjustment adopted by the FAO Conference in 1975. Commitments of external assistance for agriculture have so far reached little more than half the target level, despite the recent establishment of the International Fund for Agricultural Development (IFAD) as a financing agency exclusively for agriculture.

Providing and Coordinating External Aid

The largest single source of capital assistance for food and agriculture and for rural development is the World Bank. In recent years it has greatly increased its emphasis on these sectors, setting an example which other sources of assistance should follow.

FAO works closely with both the World Bank and IFAD in the identification and preparation of investment projects, while also providing technical assistance. An important new area for such assistance concerns the comprehensive programme being implemented by FAO to assist developing coastal States in improving and managing fish resources in the recently established exclusive economic zones.

Voluntary aid by non-governmental organisations has played an important part in meeting needs not covered by official assistance. Its flexibility and its ability to work closely with people's organisations make it an effective and creative type of assistance. The promotion of such voluntary efforts should also be a feature of World Food Day.

The Role of Trade

A large part of the export earnings of many developing countries still comes from food and other agricultural, fishery and forestry products. Whether to devote land and other resources to export crops or to food crops for domestic consumption is often a difficult choice. While export crops can provide needed or desired foreign exchange, they can create dependence on precarious world markets. The necessary imported food supplies often do not reach those who would otherwise have grown their own food. Supervision of transnational corporations under the Code of Conduct currently being developed by the United Nations would help curb those aspects of the promotion of agricultural exports which may conflict with national policies and aims.

Developing countries continue to encounter blocks to increasing their agricultural export earnings. These include protectionist measures by industrialized countries (their main markets), competition with synthetic substitutes, limited market access in the industrialised centrally planned economies, and some health and other regulations which unnecessarily affect trade in livestock products. Developing countries' share of world earnings from agricultural exports has declined dramatically. Their earnings are also highly unstable from year to year. Intergovernmental discussions and negotiations have considered these matters at length, for example in the successive rounds of Multilateral Trade Negotiations under the General Agreement on Tariffs and Trade, in the negotiations concerning UNCTAD's Integrated Programme for Commodities and a Common Fund to finance it, and in FAO's Intergovernmental Commodity Study Group. Here too progress has generally been slow. Many attempts have been made to adopt and operate international agreements between importing and exporting countries for individual commodities. Few have been agreed, even fewer have lasted very long, and the economic provisions of some have remained inoperative for long periods.

Industrialized countries need to make a number of adjustments in order to absorb the potential export surpluses of the developing countries. While adding appreciably to the export earnings of the developing countries, reductions in protection would, in turn, substantially expand their demand for the industrialized countries' exports. Such policies would also benefit consumers in the industrialized countries through lower prices.

Food Aid

Since the early 1950s, food aid has helped meet emergencies and supported nutritional programmes, food for work and development projects. Although it does not address the longer term problems of hunger and malnutrition, it is an essential interim measures.

In recent years, food aid has been on the decline. Beginning in the 1960s the United States, the world's largest exporter of grains, changed its food aid policies to place less emphasis on grants of food and much greater emphasis on foodstuffs sold at low interest and on long-term credit.

During the 1970s the total quantity of food aid decreased, not only in absolute terms but also in relation to the rapidly expanding food import requirements of the developing countries. In 1974 the World Food Conference set a minimum target of 10 million tons of cereals a year (about 0.6 per cent of annual world production). This modest amount has not yet been met. Food aid in dairy products also remains low, compared to the large surplus stocks in some nations.

Making foods available to developing nations as grants or at favourable cost deals with one aspect of their aid needs. But increases in food prices have placed an especially heavy burden on the food deficit, low income countries. The Director-General of FAO, Mr. Edouard Saouma, proposed that the International Monetary Fund provide additional support to these countries so that they can meet the rising cost of food imports, especially during time of domestic shortages. In 1981 the Fund established a new "food facility" for this purpose.

Food Stocks and Food Reserves

Food reserves can cushion the global system against devastating shortages due to crop failure or natural disasters and against excessive inflation of prices. The International Undertaking on World Food Security, which was adopted by the FAO Council in 1975, calls for the establishment of an internationally coordinated system of national reserve stocks. To date, 82 governments and the EEC have subscribed to it. It had been hoped that the Undertaking, which is voluntary, could be turned into a legally binding instrument of a new International Wheat Agreement. When the International grains negotiations broke down in February, 1979, FAO proposed a Five Point Plan of Action for implementation of the International Undertaking. While the Plan cannot substitute for a legally binding grains agreement, it encourages nations to build up stocks, and proposes criteria for managing them. It places special emphasis on the need for collective self-reliance in the developing countries themselves, through cooperative arrangements such as regional reserves. There has already been some progress in this area; for example, the Association of South East Asian Nations has established an Emergency Rice Reserve of 50,000 tons.

Another method for strengthening world food security is through the International Emergency Food Reserve of 500,000 tons of cereals a year, called for by the Seventh Special Session of the General Assembly. This target was finally met in 1981, although it is already clear that it is far from adequate.

Today cereal stocks are precariously low. The world cannot afford any major crop failures or even any natural disasters or political upheavals that would reduce yields significantly in the coming year. We should heed the important lesson taught by the experience of the early 1970s: building up adequate food reserves will help avoid famines.

Malnourishment, hunger and famine will continue to afflict human societies, and will grow worse, unless there is an informed and continuing attack on their causes and their effects. Agriculture must become a first priority in the developing world. Wherever absolute poverty exists it must be eliminated. Global trade relationship must change.

The struggle to end hunger will take many resources, and consistent effort. As a leader of those efforts FAO has worked to eradicate hunger and to bring decent living conditions to rural people. World Food Day takes another step in promoting solidarity among those involved in that struggle.

Notes and References

1. Summary by the Co-Chairman of the International Meeting on Cooperation and Development, Cancun, Mexico, 22 to 23 October, 1981.
2. Unless otherwise stated, all statistics in this booklet are based on the latest FAO data.
3. North-South: a Programme for Survival. The Report of the Independent Commission on International Development under the Chairmanship of Willy

Brandt. Pan Books, London, 1980. The Chairman of the Commission addressed the special meeting held at FAO Headquarters in Rome on 16 October, 1981 to commemorate the first World Food Day.

4. FAO. Report of the Conference of FAO, Twentieth Session, Rome, 10-28 November, 1979, Rome, 1979, p. 9.
5. All developing countries except China and other Asian centrally-planned economies.
6. FAO. World Conference on Agrarian Reform and Rural Development, Rome, 12-20 July, 1979: Report, Rome July, 1979.
7. All food deficit countries with average income per head of US$ 730 and below in 1980 (the level used by the World Bank to determine eligibility for soft-loan assistance from the International Development Association). In accordance with the guidelines and criteria agreed by the Committee on Food Aid Policies and Programmes (CFA), these countries should be given priority in the allocation of food aid.
8. FAO. *Regional Food Plan for Africa* (revised edition), Rome, 1980.
9. The United Nations system uses a variety of different classification of developing countries. The "least-developed countries" are defined as those with a per capita GDP of $ 100 or less; where the share of manufacturing in total GDP is 10 per cent or less; and where the literacy rate is 20 per cent or less.
10. FAO. *Agriculture: Towards 2000*, Rome 1981.
11. In addition to providing more development assistance and reducing trade barriers, the centrally-planned economies of the U.S.S.R. and eastern Europe could contribute greatly by solving their domestic food and agricultural problems, which are a major cause of instability at the world level.
12. FAO. Report of the Conference of FAO, Twenty-first Session, Rome, 7-25 November, 1981, p. 37-41.
13. Human Needs and Satisfactions, a global survey conducted for the Charles F. Kettering Foundation by Gallup International Research Institutes.
14. Conference Resolution 1/79, FAO, Rome, 1979.
15. Developing nations excluding China and the other Asian centrally planned economies.
16. Unless otherwise stated, the statistics quoted are based on the latest FAO data.
17. FAO. *Agriculture: Toward 2000*; Rome, 1981, p. 117
18. Ruth Leger Sivard. *World Military and Social Expenditures 1981*, World Priorities, Leesburg, Virginia, 1981, p. 3.
19. FAO. *The State of Food and Agriculture,* 1976, Rome, 1977, p. 95.
20. FAO. World Conference on Agrarian Reforms and Rural Development, Rome, 12-20 July, 1979, Report Rome, July 1979, p. 8.
21. North-South: A Programme for Survival. The Report of the Independent Commission on International Development Issues under the Chairmanship of Willy Brandt. Pan Books, London, 1980.

APPENDIX–2

FAO-IAAS STUDY (1902) ON "FOOD AND NUTRITION SECURITY IN INDIA IN 2000 AD" – ACTION PLAN

The Action Plan for attaining 'Nutrition Security in India in 2000 AD' has been developed utilising observations in the field. The Action Plan includes the following:

A. Projections of Food Demand for Nutrition Security.
B. Policy Interventions for Nutrition Security.

PROJECTIONS OF FOOD DEMAND FOR NUTRITION SECURITY

Observations at micro-level can be upgraded to provide an insight into the macro-level policies. Draft Reports were discussed by various Expert Groups to identify gaps and possible improvement in levels of consumption. For determining policy interventions the food consumption target for satisfactory level of health has been considered at a dietary energy level of 2600 calories per capita per day. 2,600 calories per capita per day has been recommended by, FAO as "Relatively Comfortable Level" (in the State of Food and Agriculture 1991). It is relevant to mention that the average global dietary energy consumption, in 1987–89, was 2700 calories per capita per day. Corresponding levels in developed countries was 3420 calories and that in developing countries was 2470 calories. It was also observed that the minimum levels recommended in our survey coincides with the higher level of agricultural production considered appropriate by the government.

India's Eighth Plan has been worked out (for the period 1992–1997) for achieving a minimum nutrition energy consumption at a low of 2300 calories per capita per day. To achieve these levels, the Planning Commission has recommended an increase in agricultural production to a level of 210 million tonnes for the year 1996-97 as compared to 172 million tonnes in 1990-91. However,

The study was conducted by IAAS in 1992 in preparation for the FAO-WHO's International Conference on Nutrition.

if the scenario for optimal nutrition standard, as recommended by our Survey, is to be achieved, the demand level will be about 240 million tonnes for the year 2000 AD. (for a population of 1 billion).

Two different Projections have been developed for Food Demand in 2000 AD. To supply 2,600 calories per capita per day. These are as follows:

Scenario I : Food Consumption Pattern to continue as at present – without consideration for 'Balanced Diet'.

Scenario II : Food Consumption Pattern to change to ensure 'Balanced Diet'.

Scenarios developed by us refer to Food Demand.

Scenario - I

This Scenario has been developed on the basis of observation that most of the dietary energy input comes from cereals in rural areas and amongst poorer sections of the people. To arrive at this scenario, observed figures of vegetables, milk, oils and fats and sugar have been considered, and balance is sought to be met through the cereals. Refer Table 1.

Scenario-I requires a minimum cereal production of 240.90 million tonnes, (rounded off to 240.00 million tonnes).

Table 1: Projection for Food Demand in 2000 AD – Scenario I

Items	Required Quantity/Capita/day (gm)	(gm)	Total Food Demand/year (million tonnes)
1. Cereals	**660**	**2279**	**240.90**
i. Wheat, Rice & Coarse Grains	610	2104	222.65
ii. Pulses	50	175	18.25
2. Vegetables	90	36	32.85
3. Milk	75	50	27.37
4. Oil & Fats	14	126	5.11
5. Sugar	35	139	12.77
6. Eggs ** (No.)	1	52	12.04 (millions)
7. Meat**	30	34	0.36
Total		2630*	

* Without dietary energy figures for eggs and meat as majority of the population is vegetarian.

** Only 30 per cent of population is considered as non-vegetarian.

Scenario-II

This scenario has been developed on the basis of recommendation on Balanced Diet by the Food & Nutrition Board Government of India. For development of projections, average figures have been worked out utilising individual recommendation for 'male' and 'female'. Recommended figures for vegetables, milk, oils and fats and sugar have been considered, and only the balance requirement is met through cereals (Table 2).

Table 2 : Projection for Food Demand in 2000 AD–Scenario II

Items	Required Quantity/Capita/day (gm)	(gm)	Total Food Demand/year (million tonnes)
1. Cereals	575	1986	209.90
i. Wheat, Rice & Coarse Grains	525	1811	191.62
ii. Pulses	50	175	18.25
2. Vegetables	180	70	65.70
3. Milk	175	117	63.87
4. Oil & Fats	35	315	12.77
5. Sugar	35	139	12.77
6. Eggs ** (No.)	1	52	12.04 (millions)
7. Meat**	30	34	0.36
Total		2629*	

* Without dietary energy figures for eggs and meat as majority of the population is vegetarian.

** Only 30 per cent of population is considered as non-vegetarian.

Scenario-II requires a minimum cereals production of 209.9 million tonnes (rounded off to 210 million tonnes). However, corresponding higher demand for vegetables, milk and oil fats will generate.

A comparison has been made amongst Present Production, VIII Five Year Plan Target; and Demand in 2000 AD. Please refer Table 3.

Table 3 : Present Food Production, VIII Five Year Plan Food Production Targets and Food Demand Projection for 2000 AD.

Items	Present 1990-91	Target 1996-97	Recommended Demand 2000 AD	
			I	II
1. Cereals	172.50	210.00	240.90	209.90
i. Wheat, Rice & Coarse Grains	158.50	193.00	222.65	191.62
ii. Pulses	14.00	17.00	18.25	18.25

It will be observed that an approach on the basis of 'Balanced Diet' is a better option to meet Food Demand in the year 2000 AD in India.

APPENDIX-3

FAO's WORLD FOOD SUMMIT (1996) – PLAN OF ACTION

Following is the text of the World Food Summit organised by FAO, at Rome in September, 1998.

1. The Rome Declaration on World Food Security and the World Food Summit Plan of Action lay the foundations of diverse paths to a common objective – food security, at the individual, household, national, regional and global levels. Food security exists when all people, at all times, have physical and economic access to sufficient, safe and nutritious food to meet their dietary needs and food preferences for an active and healthy life. In this regard, concerted action at all levels is required. Each nation must adopt a strategy consistent with its resources and capacities to achieve its individual goals and, at the same time, cooperate regionally and internationally in order to organize collective solutions to global issues of food security. In a world of increasingly interlinked institutions, societies and economies, coordinated efforts and shared responsibilities are essential.
2. Poverty eradication is essential to improve access to food. The vast majority of those who are undernourished, either cannot produce or cannot afford to buy enough food. They have inadequate access to means of production such as land, water, inputs, improved seeds and plants, appropriate technologies and farm credit. In addition, wars, civil strife, natural disasters, climate related ecological changes and environmental degradation have adversely affected millions of people. Although food assistance may be provided to ease their plight, it is not a long-term solution to the underlying causes of food insecurity. It is important to

FAO's World Summit at Rome in September, 1998.

maintain an adequate capacity in the international community to provide food aid, whenever it is required, in response to emergencies. Equitable access to stable food supplies should be ensured.

3. A peaceful and stable environment in every country is a fundamental condition for the attainment of sustainable food security. Governments are responsible for creating an enabling environment for private and group initiatives to devote their skills, efforts and resources, and in particular investment, towards the common goal of food for all. This should be undertaken with the cooperation and participation of all members of society. Farmers, fishers and foresters and other food producers and providers, have critical roles in achieving food security, and their full involvement and enablement are crucial for success.

4. Poverty, hunger and malnutrition are some of the principal causes of accelerated migration from rural to urban areas in developing countries. The largest population shift of all times is now under way. Unless these problems are addressed in an appropriate and timely fashion, the political economic and social stability of many countries and regions may well be seriously affected, perhaps even compromising world peace. It is necessary to target those people and areas suffering most from hunger and malnutrition and identify causes and take remedial action to improve the situation. A more complete, user-friendly sources of information at all levels would enable this.

5. Availability of enough food for all can be attained. The 5.8 billion people in the world today have, on average, 15 per cent more food per person than the global population of 4 billion people and 20 years ago. Yet, further large increases in world food production, through the sustainable management of natural resources, are required to feed a growing population, and achieve improved diets. Increased production, including traditional crops and their products, in efficient combination with food imports, reserves, and international trade can strengthen food security and address

regional disparities. Food aid is one of the many instruments in research and in cataloguing and conserving genetic resources, particularly at the national level, i.e. essential. The link between sufficient food supplies and household food security must be ensured.

6. Harmful seasonal and inter-annual instability of food supplies can be reduced. Progress should include targeting on minimising the vulnerability to, and impact of, climate fluctuations and pests and diseases. To effect timely transfers of supplies to deficit areas and the conservation and sustainable use of biodiversity, use should be made, in efficient combination, of climate early warning systems, transfer and utilization of appropriate agricultural, fishery and forestry technologies, production, and reliable trade, storage and financial mechanisms. Natural and man-made disasters can often be anticipated or even prevented, and response must be timely and effective and assist recovery.

7. Unless national governments and the international community address the multifaceted causes underlying food insecurity, the number of hungry and malnourished people will remain very high in developing countries, particularly in Africa south of the Sahara; and sustainable food security will not be achieved. This situation is unacceptable. This Plan of Action envisaged an ongoing effort to eradicate hunger in all countries, with an immediate view to reducing the number of undernourished people to half their present level not later than 2015, and a mid-term review to ascertain whether it is possible to achieve this target by 2010.

8. The resources required for investment will be generated mostly from domestic, private and public sources. The international community has a key role to play in supporting the adoption of appropriate national policies and, where necessary and appropriate, in providing technical and financial assistance to assist developing countries and countries with economies in transition in fostering food security.

9. The multi-dimensional nature of the flow-up to the World

Food Summit includes actions at the national, inter-governmental and inter-agency levels. The international community, and the UN system, including FAO, as well as other agencies and bodies according to their mandates, have important contributions to the implementation of the World Food Summit Plan of Action. The FAO Committee on World Food Security (CFS) will have responsibility to monitor the implementation of the Plan of Action.

10. Reaching sustainable World Food Security is part and parcel of achieving the social, economic, environmental and human development objectives agreed upon in recent international conferences. The World Food Summit Plan of Action builds on consensus reached in these fora and is based on the conviction that although the world is faced with major food insecurity, solutions to these problems exist. If all parties at local, national, regional and international levels make determined and sustained efforts, then the overall goal of food for all, at all times, will be achieved.

11. The Plan of Action of the World Food Summit is in conformity with the purposes and principles of the UN Charter and international laws and strives to consolidate the results of other UN conferences since 1990 on subjects have a bearing on food security.

12. The implementation of recommendations contained in this Plan of Action is the sovereign right and responsibility of each State through national laws and the formulation of strategies, policies, programmes, and development priorities, in conformity with all human rights and fundamental freedoms, including the right to development, and the significance of and the full respect of various religious and ethical values, cultural backgrounds and philosophical convictions of individuals and their communities should contribute to the full enjoyment by all of their human rights in order to achieve the objective of food security for all.

APPENDIX-4

ISSUES IN RURAL POVERTY, EMPLOYMENT AND FOOD SECURITY IN THE CONTEXT OF THE WORLD SUMMIT FOR SOCIAL DEVELOPMENT

INTRODUCTION

800 million of the world's 1.1 billion poor live in rural areas. Yet in many developing countries the rural sector continues to suffer from neglect and, indeed, exploitation mainly to the benefit of urban interests. Available resources have been used for investments in industry and services, maintenance of the civil service, improvement of urban infrastructures and living conditions. This leaves the poor in rural areas with little hope of breaking out of the poverty trap.

Developing nations are also confronted with a difficult and constraining international environment. This includes structural adjustment programmes which take scant account of the limits imposed by their agriculture-based economies, unstable markets for most of their exports, and increasing international competition (following the Uruguay Round agreement) for their fledging industries and weak farm economies; a debt burden built up largely as a result of declining terms of trade and loans for economic projects which have failed to bring in the planned returns.

The rural poor depend directly or indirectly on agriculture for employment and incomes; boosting the rural economy, in particular by sustainably raising food and agricultural production, is therefore, one of the chief means of alleviating poverty and rural unemployment. Because the rural poor constitute a large part of the global social problem, it is important that they should become part of the solution. For the rural sector today plays not only an economic but also a social role, by commission and by omission. By commission, it provides food and employment for a substantial

---

Paper presented by FAO at the World Summit for Social Development in 1995.

share of the population and this role can be greatly expanded. By omission, it leaves many without employment and living on the brink of survival.

So long as the returns on agricultural production remains so low, it will be virtually impossible for agriculture to compete for capital with industry and services. But if the hidden social cost of maintaining agriculture in its present parlous state – massive waste of human resources, cost of curative rural health care, environmental destruction (the ecological and social aspects meet here), unbalanced spread of population between rural and urban areas, growing social problems in the cities – were included in the equation, the real cost to developing countries' economies would become much clearer. Investing in the sustainable development of the potential of agriculture, forestry and fisheries will cost much less in the longer term than solving the social problems which rural neglect is generating.

The secular neglect of agriculture reflects the low value placed in the past on natural resources. The growing recognition of their importance and fragility provides another strong argument for investing more in agriculture, fisheries and forestry, and for compensating agricultural producers for their role and responsibility as providers of food security and custodians of natural resources.

Increasing food production is a necessary but not sufficient condition for solving hunger and poverty. World food production per capita was 18 per cent higher in 1990 than 30 years earlier and according to one calculation, current production of cereals, roots and tubers, pulses and vegetables in 91 developing countries is sufficient to feed their population of 2.8 billion...provided it were equitably shared. Making the link between production and food security entails a whole process of marketing and distribution, at the end of which there must be consumers with effective purchasing power. So long as the poor are deprived of the means to generate incomes to purchase food, or of resources to produce for their needs, they will remain hungry. How the share access to productive resources equitably is a major concern of the World Summit on Social Development.

Summoning up the necessary political will to apply rural development policies aimed at boosting the agricultural economy and improving rural living, especially for the rural poor – in the face of resistance by human and economic interests such as local elites, bureaucrats, economic groupings, the military – is without doubt the most difficult task facing governments. This would be made easier if a broad-based alliance behind such a policy could be forged. Apparently opposing actors, including the poor themselves, would support policies for poverty alleviation (which would free human capital and lead to an enlargement of the market), raising national food production, and stemming the rate of growth of the cities, if they could be motivated by enlightened self-interest.

The central theme of the Summit will be poverty. Because of the lack of prospects and amenities in rural areas, the rural poor are flocking to the towns. Many find little respite there so that their flight simply transfers rural poverty to the urban areas, creating squalor and even more despair and providing a breeding ground for political and religious extremism and violence. Urban groups, including the poor, are more visible and thus command more of their governments' attention. But the solution to the mushrooming urban problems is intimately tied up with solving the rural problems. In turn, urban poverty leads to northward migration, spurred on by imaging of opulence relayed by the mass media.

At the end of the 20th Century, the developed countries themselves are today contending with situations which are beginning to mirror those of the South: destruction of the environment (now beginning to be remedied), high rates of unemployment, break-down of social structures, a growing class of marginalized urban poor, ineffectiveness of certain classical economic remedies in solving social problems. Perhaps these parallels can provide the building blocks for North/South alliances and the kind of global solidarity against poverty and marginalisation called for the Summit.

The overall problems related to sustainable agriculture and rural development (SARD) have been dealt with substantially at the 1991 den Bosch Conference (1) and in Chapter XIV of Agenda 21 adopted at the 1992 UNCED. Nevertheless, the Social Summit

should address the main issues related to rural poverty.[1]
Three issues seem to be currently of particular importance:

- how to overcome current constraints on boosting food production for local consumption;
- how to pursue policies for social equity and sustainable development in the face of international constraints such as the weight of the debt burden, structural adjustment and the new world trade rules.
- how to feed the exponentially growing populations of the cities.

The document looks first at the enabling environment for rural poverty alleviation and then raises some questions regarding rural poverty and employment.

AN ENABLING ENVIRONMENT FOR RURAL POVERTY ALLEVIATION

Reversing Past Economic Policy Trends

Reversing the neglect which the rural sector has suffered from in most countries requires fundamental changes of policy and resource allocation: macro-economic policies that will stimulate the rural economy, agricultural policies and accompanying measures to boost food production for local consumption, and institutional arrangements to guarantee that all actors have a voice and have access to resources.

In many countries, agricultural producers, rich and poor alike, were long burdened with heavy taxation (e.g. taxes on marketed cash crops). Urban consumers benefited from subsidies on basic foods, and from cheap imports. The rural rich benefited from subsidies on inputs and machinery which the poor do not typically use in large amounts. The insidious effects of this bias have been mainly felt by the poorest segments of rural communities. Today,

[1] See the den Bosch Declaration and Agenda for Action on SARD. FAO/ Netherlands Government Conference on Sustainable Agriculture and Rural Development, 's-Hertogenbosch, The Netherlands, April 1991.

increasing numbers of countries are making corrections to this situation.

Considerable further progress is needed to eliminate such distortions. Correcting them is one objective of structural adjustment programmes (SAPs). SAPs as conceived and often applied negatively impact on the poor (reduction in social services, elimination on subsidies, more open competition from imports without proper preparation of national markets, sudden currency devaluation). Nonetheless, structural adjustment cannot be considered undesirable *per se*. The question is, what should SAPs be aiming at, how to take due account of the constraints of agriculture-based economies (in particular the steep fluctuations in incomes and budgetary resources which can make precise planning virtually impossible), what measures should they include, what should be the time-scale of their implementation, and how can their negative effects on social well-being, the environment and indeed on production be reduced[2]? People-friendly structural adjustment is part of the enabling environment; associating representatives of all social sectors with the design of SAPs is a way of minimising their negative impact.

Agricultural policies in most developing countries have concentrated mainly on *cash crop* production for export. This pre-independence objective has been largely maintained since independence. Most public, and all private company research has been cash-crop oriented; extension services have likewise concentrated on crops with a high market potential which, moreover, occupy the most productive land. With the advent of high-yielding hybrid cereals, such as rice, maize and wheat, leading to the so-called Green Revolution, such major cereals also gained attention in high-potential areas benefiting from relatively little attention.

The evolution of markets for most cash crops has hardly justified such policy bias. To provide but two examples, in 1991,

2. UNICEF estimates that only around 10 per cent of national budgets are spent on social amenities (education, health, water, sanitation....). The share of that which reaches the rural areas, and more especially the poor, is negligible in many countries. It is inconceivable that such a low level of social support should be further reduced under SAPs.

prices of coffee and tea in real terms were at their lowest level since 1950; the fall in prices of Africa's export commodities between 1986 and 1990 has been estimated to have cost the continent $ 50 billion in lost revenues.

There is strong case today for concentrating more attention and resources on food crops for local consumption, especially in low-income food deficit countries.

Empowering the Poor

Guaranteeing a voice for the poor is no easy task. Many attempts over the years have failed: cooperatives have been turned into instruments of the rich and of governments, peasant revolts have been quelled, vocal leaders have been silenced. There is no reason to assume that the poor will find it easier to organise in the future than in the past.

At local level, traditional community management of resources has weakened. National and expatriate NGOs have an increasingly strong record in reviving community organizations and validating community management of resources. In this, NGOs have several comparative advantages, including their presence at grassroots level, their capacity to promote innovative approaches supporting rural people's own initiatives, and their experience in applying participatory approaches.

Recent experience has shown that constructive dialogue can be established between organised small producers and the authorities. Community management and local and national dialogue are gaining increasing importance, as governments' outreach capacity becomes more limited due to lack of resources and the limitations of structural adjustment.

Decentralisation and a transformation of the function of the State from a directive to a facilitator role could contribute strongly for creating a favourable environment: by devolving functions such as marketing, extension, storage, transport and credit onto private and community institutions, governments will free scarce human and financial resources which can be applied more effectively to building infrastructures, providing services for the very poor with no means to pay, correcting the failures and shortcomings of the market, ensuring that legislation is effectively applied and creating the conditions for fledgling people-based economic organisations to operate efficiently in the face of better-established privately-owned organisations. Care must be taken to ensure that the transfer from the public to the private sector is gradual and smooth, otherwise there could be a damaging disruption in services which would probably affect the poor most. It would be wrong to assume that the private sector is by definition efficient, any more than NGOs are infallible.

RURAL POVERTY AND EMPLOYMENT

As agriculture became less self-sufficient (increasing use of purchased inputs, for example), and the monetary economy spread, rural poverty has tended to increase. The monetary gains to be had from intensifying the production process tempted many larger producers to expand acreage to the detriment of the poor, without necessarily raising demand for farm labour. Population growth is also playing an undeniable role: the world population is projected to grow to 7.2 billion by 2010, of which 80 per cent will be in developing countries compared to 76 per cent in 1990.

Causes of Rural Poverty

The phenomenon of rural poverty is complex and varies considerably within and between countries and, indeed, over time. Among its major causes are inadequate and inequitable access to productive resources such as land, water, fisheries, forests, credit, energy.

Lack of agricultural or off-farm income-earning opportunities[3] is another major cause of rural poverty. As a result of factors such as low prices for farm output, the depressed state of the rural economy in most countries, and poor transport and market infrastructures, combined with a rapidly-expanding rural population, there is simply not enough remunerated work to go round. On the other hand, during

3. In sub-Saharan Africa, over 50 per cent of the rural labour force is under-employed (*see* Social Summit Prep Com: Expert meeting on the Expansion of Productive Employment, November 1993.

seasonal peaks in demand, there can be shortages of agricultural labour.

Neglect of the crops, production systems and survival strategies of the poor has contributed in various ways to rural poverty. The introduction of higher-yielding varieties and the technological packages which have accompanied them, especially in Asia, has led to a loss of biodiversity, especially rustic varieties, which in turn has contributed to greater food insecurity for the poor (low drought and disease resistance of high-yielding varieties)[4]. Modern cultivation methods have also had poverty-inducing side effects such as drastically reducing numbers of many plants used for medicinal purposes which are seen as "weeds" under the technological packages.

The introduction of non-indigenous technologies has also affected employment opportunities: while some technologies are labour-replacing (mechanisation of sugarcane harvesting), others are labour-creating (intensification through, for instance, integrated crop and livestock systems, multi-cropping, integrated pest management). New technologies often have a more negative effect on female labour (increased drudgery, greater work load, or alternatively loss of employment), the men mainly benefiting from its positive effects.

These disadvantages are compounded by poor distribution systems both for farm products, inputs and consumer goods, and by restricted access to public services (education, health care, family planning, old age care) and the quality of these services. Extension services and communications tend to be not only weak and commodity-specific but frequently irrelevant to the concerns of the poor, and the urban bias in formal education which, when available, is usually ill-adapted to the needs of rural living.

The increasingly problematic access to energy supplies essential for cooking, especially wood, but also energy needed for

4. A typical example can be found in Zimbabwe where farmers were purchasing hybrid seeds from large companies but these did not include sorghum and millet well adapted to drought conditions; they are now producing and distributing their own seed through a national NGO: a good example of private initiative working in farmers' interests. See DEEP, FAO, 1994.

domestic lighting and mechanised agriculture (pumps, rural industry), combined with the inability of the poor to pay for commercial energy such as kerosene, and the technical difficulties of introducing alternative energies provide another slant to the rural poverty trap.

The Consequences of Rural Poverty

Three main consequences of rural poverty can be highlighted.

- The first is food insecurity[5], since of all human needs food is the most basic. The lack of access to regular supplies of food for a balanced diet is compounded by the pressure to sell, rather than consume, high-value food products such as fruit, milk and meat. Inadequate and unbalanced diets, and lack of clean water determine poor health and disease which, in turn, reduces the capacity of the poor to work productively.
- Depletion of natural resources and environmental damage are also consequences of rural poverty as the poor are forced, by population pressure and lack of access to productive lands, to cultivate fragile marginal land (especially communal land), overgraze pastures, and destroy forest resources and coastal fisheries in a desperate effort to survive in the short-term which in turn aggravates their changes of survival in the longer term. But the poors are far from being the only causes of environmental damage; modern agriculture in both the South and the North, has resulted in soil erosion, water pollution, loss of biodiversity.
- Rural out-migration by the poor, mainly male in the first stage, is essentially provoked by poverty results in a "feminization" of the countryside, but also of poverty, and depopulation by able-bodied rural males, especially the young and educated, raising the real spectre in some areas of absolute shortages of rural labour. Massive urbanization[6] with the attendant problems

5. The ultimate objective of World Food Security was defined by FAO in 1983 as follows: "to ensure that all people at all times have both physical and economic access to the basic food they need".
6. The urban population of the developing countries is projected by the United Nations to grow from less than 1 billion (29 per cent of those countries' population) in 1980 to 2.7 billion (47 per cent) in 2010 – only 16 years from now.

of feeding the impoverished and even more fragile urban underclass and increasing economic and social problems (violence, insecurity, spreading right into the "rich" neighbourhoods) in the urban areas. Feeding that population from domestic sources and imports will be a major problem of the 21st Century.

Solution and Constraints

The solutions to these chronic difficulties are well-documented. The crunch comes when putting them into practice. In other words, we know what to do, but rarely how to do it in the face of economic, political and social realities.

Promoting overall rural development, will help the less-poor, but will it also have positive spin-offs for the rural poor? Will a dynamic rural economy stimulate demand for non-farm services, goods produced in urban centres, and therefore jobs? Is this the "trickle-down" theory revisited? In situations where total resources are limited, *inter alia* due to servicing the foreign debt, how will governments manage to reduce any particular allocation and overcome the objections of some entitlement holders (the military) who are more sensitive than others (social services). Where decisions are tied up in structural adjustment and "market mechanism" straight-jackets, enhancing agricultural prices and turning the terms of trade in favour of the sector can be problematic and slow. Higher food prices will lead to increased urban improvement and unrest. These are the types of constraints governments must face up to.

Non-farm employment (processing, rural services, metal-working, cottage industries) is increasing rapidly in some countries such as China and South-East Asia, thus relieving rural poverty. But it may be further aggravating agricultural labour shortages where they exist since non-far jobs tend to be better paid, making workers reluctant to accept agricultural employment when non-farm jobs are available.

Food processing provides a means of creating jobs and retaining value added in the rural areas. Research should seek ways of overcoming the problems of perishability and processing associated with many local food crops; such shortcomings lead to considerable waste and make local foods less attractive for city dwellers. Improvements to the safety and quality of such foods is also needed.

So long as absolute poverty exists in rural areas, public works programmes aimed at building necessary infrastructures (roads, bridges, markets), and soil and water conservation for example, will have a role to play. Should food aid as part-payment of wages be used in such programmes or confined to emergency situations? While public works create temporary jobs, a proper balance must be found between their job-creating and infrastructure-creating function. Is it feasible to plan and implement public works programmes with the participation of the local people? This may be a way of ensuring that public works solve problems identified by them so that they will ensure management and maintenance once the programme is over.

For the poor to gain equitable access to resources control must be wrested from those who control them inequitably now, including private citizens and State agencies. Land and water are major resources. Can access be enhanced through applying land reforms and legislation on pasture, forest and water users' rights and obligations? Is experience so far encouraging? In the past, community management of water, pastures, forests and coastal fisheries has traditionally been widespread. In some cases, these systems are breaking down for social or economic reasons, or being undermined by privatisation policies.

Credit is another essential resource the poors are often deprived of. Are informal credit systems a viable solution? Has NGO experience been successful in promoting informal credit? What lessons have been learned?

Is positive discrimination needed to provide rural women with access to productive resources, credit and education? Their growing burden in terms of food and agricultural production, family survival and protection of the environment seems to justify such discrimination. Policies, training and extension services must be gender-sensitive.

In vertical expansion of production of typically poor people's crops and livestock a viable option for expanding production and employment while limiting resource destruction? To what degree can the synergism between traditional and modern technologies (e.g. maximizing crop rotation, green manuring, organic pest control, judicious use of chemical fertilizers) be exploited to this end? Such combinations can be more labour-intensive and environment-friendly.

What role can agricultural research play in addressing food security objectives and poverty relief (e.g. raising sustainable productivity of marginal or resource-poor areas such as arid or mountainous areas, boosting yields of local food crops, improving and rehabilitating ecologically sound traditional practices). What experience have NGOs gained in this area? Technical assistance should accompany existing practices and built on people's knowledge, experience and production strategies. To what degree can their limitations be addressed through scientific knowledge of agriculture and agro-ecology?

What experience have NGOs in associating rural people with technology development in areas such as agroforestry, soil and water conservation, and biodiversity.

The first Green Revolution increased food output but with some considerable negative side-effects (loss of biodiversity, increased rural poverty among the landless, marginalisation of important crops such as pulses, soil erosion, depletion or salinization of groundwater).[7] The new Green Revolution must be environmentally sensitive, food-crop oriented and socially acceptable. According to FAO, there is a large potential to raise average farmer yields considerably for many important crops. What is needed to tap that potential?

In view of the concern for sustainability and environmental protection raised by modern agricultural techniques, should more prominence be given to "softer" technologies using knowledge-based management practices in which information will play an important role (fewer new large-scale irrigation systems, more low-cost, user-managed and efficient water harvesting and use; less

7. See Vandana Shiva: The Violence of the Green Revolution.

chemical fertilizer, more recourse to integrated plant nutrition systems and soil conservation measures; less pesticides, more integrated pest management)? Would this be a means of enlarging the place of traditional, holistic practices? What experience have NGOs gained of farmer-to-farmer exchanges (the way farmer-invented techniques have always been shared) and what are the conditions of success?

Moving to such a new system will require a good dose of humility on the part of national and expatriate "experts", recognizing the value of local knowledge and wisdom of traditional practices and of the complex and multiple survival strategies of the poor.

General education and skills training are essential to prepare rural people in particular for non-farm jobs. Investing in general education is now recognized as giving high returns; "Education is the key to develop the individual's capability to adapt to changing circumstances. A good general education...introduces communication, abstract reasoning and problem-solving skills...", in the words of the Expert Meeting on the Expansion of Productive Employment, convened as a contribution to the Social Summit. What training approaches can best provide small farmers with the ability to discuss the relative merits of various tehnological options? What can be done to overcome the lack of trained and skilled teachers, and the unwillingness of staff to relocate to outlying areas? What can be done to make urban-biased curricula, ill-adapted to rural living, more relevant?

International assistance activities should devote more resources to countries facing particularly difficult conditions due to unfavourable resource endowments: the Low-Income Food Deficit Countries. What change have they, without long-term outside help, of surmounting their poverty and food insecurity problems? How can the insensitivity of much foreign assistance to local needs and more especially to the cultural differences in third world societies be corrected? How can development assistance programmes be refocused on the real problem and become more realistic in their expectations (more stress on subtle social transformation and less on quick economic returns)? Project activities have too often been geared to high-tech solutions opening up lucrative contracts of engineering and construction companies in the home country (large dams, nuclear power stations, sophisticated farm machinery). The massive third world debt is one of the most striking consequences of this type of wrong "development". Is there room for a public campaign in the North explaining that so-called "assistance" to the South has rarely been altruistic and should henceforth result in a net transfer of resources adapted to local needs and controlled by the beneficiaries?

Last but far from least, what support is needed by people's organizations and other representative rural institutions in order to gain an effective voice? How can current power structures be convinced that dialogue is in their interest? Does social stratification (by gender, caste and tribe, rich and poor, cultivator and livestock raiser...) which usually determines village power structures constitute an insurmountable obstacle to empowerment of the poor and the weak? What is the NGOs' experience in the field? Over the years, by overuse and abuse, the notion of "people's participation" may have become somewhat devalued. Do the concepts of social responsibility and accountability of the authorities to the community provide a basis for participation to regain substance and meaning based on local cultural values?

Within the context of representation, particular mention must finally be made of the institutional and social systems which lead to the social alienation of poor rural women, usually the main victims of neglect and poverty. The burden women already bear is aggravated by male rural exodus, which leaves women to shoulder "male" as well as "female" responsibilities in societies which are not geared to women-headed households (30 per cent of rural households in Africa). How can this incapacitation of women, which constitutes a massive waste of human resources, be overcome? Can poor rural women's roles be valorised and recognized by legislation, including rights to property, civil rights and family rights, in order to allow them to develop their potential? While growing understanding of their roles and the constraints they face is leading to more effective interventions in their favour, there is a very long way still to go.

CONCLUSION

There may be developing, around the themes of the Summit, a convergence of interests between the NGOs community and new options being adopted by FAO. The first two major issues outlined in the introduction – food production for local consumption, international effects on poverty and food security – have long been of special concern to development and advocacy NGOs alike. The third – how to feed the cities of the South – will be a growing problem during the coming decades.

FAO is convinced that many countries of the South, including in Africa, have the potential to raise their agricultural production and in doing so, to contribute to poverty alleviation (through job creation) as well as to raising food production. But there is no magic wand to make this come about. Complex economic, social and biophysical factors will have to be combined and these combinations constantly reviewed. The NGO community is already contributing strongly to reflexions and actions on these equations. FAO has technical and policy experience, both positive and negative, on which to call. Small farmers, their community organizations, NGOs, governments and international organizations should join forces to bring about the needed changes.

Properly conceived and implemented structural adjustment programmes could contribute to a more healthy economic environment for constructive change in urban and rural areas. But agreement on the contents of such programmes, and their operation, may be difficult to achieve. A more open world trading system would allow the countries of the South to compete fairly on international markets. However, the Uruguay Round agreement may have negative effects, for some of the poorest countries of the South (difficulty in competing on world markets without preferential treatment, higher prices for imported foods, ban on domestic price measures). The expected rise in world cereals prices should raise producer prices for these and similar staples. But the urban and rural consumers who have no production capability will be penalised.

Besides, there are those who feel that in promoting (free)

market economics, it is too often forgotten that the conditions for markets to operate efficiently are not in fact fulfilled. World markets for major commodities exported from the South (from cocoa and tea to tobacco and medicinal plants) are subject to "olygopsonies" (a few large purchasers, mainly transitional companies). National markets are far from operating openly since some operators have privileged access to information which should be generally available. So long as this situation continues – and it is unlikely to be changed either by the Uruguay Round or by SAPs – it will be unrealistic to expect the announced benefits of market mechanisms to accrue.

Finally, the problems associated with the rapid growth of the cities of the South are only just beginning to be addressed. Many countries may not be in a position to earn enough from agricultural or industrial production and services to be able to purchase on world markets the food they are unable to produce from their own resources. Food aid will certainly not suffice, even if it were a viable option. Stepping up their own production, while technically feasible for many countries, poses many problems alluded to above. What can be done to prepare for this looming problem of the 21st Century?

APPENDIX-5

WORLD FOOD DAY - 1998—REPORT

ROUND TABLE
ON
PANCHAYATI RAJ AND FOOD SECURITY :
OPPORTUNITY FOR WOMEN'S PARTICIPATION

REPORT

A National Consultation on "Panchayati Raj and Food Security: Opportunity for Women's Participation was organised jointly by the IAAS and the FAO on October 15, 1998 to celebrate World Food Day 1998. WFD Awards to media personnel were also presented on the occasion.

Dr. N.C. Saxena, Secretary, Ministry of Rural Areas and Employment, Government of India was the Chief Guest at the Inaugural Session and presented the World Food Day Awards and Dr. M.S. Swaminathan, President, M.S. Swaminathan Research Foundation was the Chairman of the Round Table Consultation.

ROUND TABLE CONSULTATION

Mr. Peter Rosenegger, FAO Representative in India welcomed the participants on behalf of FAO and deliberated on the concept of the World Food Day and the TeleFood programme introduced by the DG, FAO. Mr. Rosenegger said that realising the importance of the third tier of governance in India, efforts have been supported by the FAO to evolve a mechanism for ensuring food security through the delivery mechanism of Panchayats. "Women Feed the World" being the theme of the year helps us to focus on the opportunities for women's participation in attaining Food Security.

Mr. Rosenegger mentioned of the efforts made by FAO, Ministry of Rural Areas and Employment and the Rural Development Department of Government of Maharashtra in developing a Project for UNDP funding for setting up a Model

Panchayat System. He mentioned that the discussion will be focused on the same.

Dr. K.P.A. Menon, President, IAAS in his welcome address said that, The Indian Association for the Advancement of Science has the privilege of celebrating the World Food Day in collaboration with the FAO, since its inception in 1981. During this long cooperation, the Association had the opportunity to involve with a number of issues of interest to FAO at the National, Regional and International levels. The World Food Day Awards were instituted, jointly by the IAAS and FAO, to recognise contributions of distinguished scientists/experts and mass media personnel to disseminate information and create awareness about issues relating to rural development and agriculture, food and nutrition.

Mr. Mohan Kandha, Jt. Secretary, Ministry of Agriculture and Cooperation, Government of India and the Convener of the National Committee on World Food Day appreciated the efforts of organising a National Consultation as part of the World Food Day. Mr. Kandha mentioned that Panchayats now have important role in the national governance and need to be fully utilised for ensuring various social and economic development activities for the rural poor. He indicated that the Ministry of Agriculture has also realised that certain gaps have to be covered in its extension services and considers that the Panchayati Raj system can implement food security related programmes much more effectively. He mentioned that the initiative of Government of Maharashtra may prove a fore runner to the revolution of food security through panchayat governance.

Ms. Brenda McSweeney, Resident Coordinator in India, UNDP in her address mentioned of the UNDP's framework programme focusing on poverty alleviation and food security. Various elements under this programme have direct relationship with the Panchayats. The pro-poor programme of the UNDP is aimed at Panchayats helping in alleviating poverty and hunger. She mentioned also of the work of Dr. Amartya Sen on welfare economic and its impact on UNDP's working. She emphasised that under food security and pro-poor sub-programmes for India, specific request of the

Government of Maharashtra can certainly find a place.

She mentioned that GEF support programme in the field of bio-diversity also has a number of elements crucial to attaining food security. At the end she mentioned that Dr. Amartya Sen considered women as agent of social change and it would be the best tribute to him if we focus on women in the same spirit.

Dr. N.C. Saxena, Secretary, Ministry of Rural Areas and Employment in his inaugural address mentioned three themes, in relation to Food Security and Panchayati Raj. These are: Food Security, Panchayati Raj; and Women. He said that farming is no longer a household activity and nor can be developed only by government support. Role of the private sector is equally important. The capital intensity in agriculture in India should be proportionate to the urban population. USA with 98 per cent urbanisation should be expected to make capital intensity at 98 per cent. The capital intensity in India, making it proportionate to urban population, should make agriculture capital intensive to only upto 30 per cent. The capital intensity of agriculture should be reduced and the labour intensity should be intensified. In times to come, the unit for Food Security should not be household but the whole village as a composite unit and that is where the role of Panchayats become important.

Panchayats are searching for a role model. An ideal model of decision making will be the one which will be diffused in action and every member will be willing to take action and responsibility. Governments in a few States like, Madhya Pradesh, Kerala, Tamil Nadu and Andhra Pradesh have strengthened village Panchayats to get social development work executed through them.

Women can play a constructive role if they have the land rights. So far, the land rights have been a major constraint in enhanced women's contribution to rural development. The Ministry has asked every State to re-examine the case. Dr. Saxena appreciated the Secretary, Rural Development, Government of Maharashtra for developing a Model Project in consultation with his Ministry.

Mrs. Sudha Pillai, Jt. Secretary, Ministry of Rural Areas and Employment said that liberalisation of economy and Panchayati

Raj may result in a revolution any change in the national social and economic sectors. Gram Panchayats already find a place in the national planning process. A great majority of panchayats are becoming important and powerful. States are also realising that empowerment of panchayats will be important for speedy development of rural masses. Some of the States like Rajasthan are now giving more powers to Panchayats.

There are certain salient points which indicated as to what has not been done and a few of them can be summarised as follows :

(i) Panchayats are not given powers to work outside rural development departments.

(ii) Various other departments have 30-40 schemes of rural development that do not find a mention in the working of Panchayats.

(iii) The Central Government does not deal with anyone below the level of Secretary of the State Government.

(iv) By-and large very little effort has been made by States to devolve power at the Panchayat level.

Panchayats have come to stay; and a number of UN agencies like FAO, UNICEF, UNESCO and UNDP, have their programmes oriented at women, and their involvement in Panchayats. It may be helpful to organise workshops in the rural areas to create awareness amongst the beneficiaries. That will also help in building technical competence and skills of the panchayat functionaries.

Women have a special role in improving nutrition. Unfortunately women do not own even two per cent of land and do not have a say in the decision making. The situation is improving but it will take time before a revolution takes place. It is necessary that convergence takes place in the activities of different departments. Unless that happens, the Panchayats will find difficult to transfer the benefits at the village level.

It may be most appropriate for FAO to look into the region of Mewat in Haryana and some of the blocks in Uttar Pradesh. A pilot project can be launched with a view to support the nutrition status.

Ms. Pillai appreciated the efforts of Government of Maharashtra to develop a Model Project for Panchayats' involvement in food security.

Mr. Ramesh Kumar, Secretary, Department of Rural Development and Water Conservation, Government of Maharashtra presented a Concept of the Project titled "Food Security and Panchayati Raj – The Maharashtra Project Model for Consideration under the UN Funding Mechanism".

For designing the project model, lessons have been drawn from the IFAD assisted Maharashtra Rural Credit Project (MRCP) being implemented in the State. MRCP is based on a rural micro credit strategy and Women's Self Help Group (MSHG). There is great emphasis on social mobilisation of rural community. MRCP is being implemented in conjunction with the UNICEF sponsored development philosophy entitled community action. The project proposal for UN assistance is geared to complement the ongoing Maharashtra State Government Schemes.

Project has been suggested for two tribal blocks of Dharni in Amravati district and Mokhade in Thane district.

The *Project goal* has been defined as "To Empower Tribal Village Panchayats to take collaborative action for ameliorating the nutritional and food deprivation prevailing in their communities".

"The *major project objective* is to develop village panchayat level strategies for augmenting the nutritional and food security status through collaborative community action; and to empower the village panchayat for development and monitor action plan for food security."

Salient features of the project model and the project activities were also presented.

Dr. M.S. Swaminathan, in his remarks mentioned that "food security concept, as applied presently at the household level, needs to be redefined and our focus should shift to single person base. He said that the availability of food in the market is not a problem. Economic access is the real problem which calls for creating non-formal employment avenues. It should also be remembered that the absorption of food is the second issue in food security and depends on safe drinking water and environmental conditions. The

National Agenda on Governance also emphasises on "hunger free" country programme which needs to be emphasised".

Panchayats have *seven basic* elements relating to Food Security. The first is that it should be left to the people to identify as to who are hungry and malnourished. Entitlement to the people is the second most important aspect. The third issue is that the protein calorie malnutrition has been a major concern for the masses in India. The fourth issue is hidden hunger and relates to micro nutrition deficiency. Besides, absorption and retention is a reflection of a person's general physical condition and this is the fifth important aspect. Livelihood resulting in economic access to food is the sixth important element, and relates directly to employment creation. The seventh concern is the focus on nutrition status of pregnant women and children.

Dr. Swaminathan lamented that the women's programmes are basically add-on projects. As a matter of fact, women's livelihood projects should be related to reducing the drudgery mainly in terms of number of working hours.

Dr. Swaminathan complimented Mr. Ramesh Kumar for his Project outline and supported its immediate funding and implementation under UNDP/FAO.

Dr. Kamal Islam, Nutrition Expert, UNICEF mentioned that the most important aspect is communication to bring around behavioural change and to improve community's nutritional status. He said that the issue of invisibility has not been mentioned at all. The existing situation in India indicates that the number of malnutritioned has increased, but the people of fourth degree malnutrition are now less or one can say missing. This means a qualitative change has taken place in our system. Nutrition education has to be introduced to bring around attitudinal change in the masses.

Dr. G.C. Shrotriya, Senior Manager, (Bio-sciences), IFFCO, mentioned that focus on the community land has brought around significant improvement in nutritional status. At the village level a number of cooperatives exist as also the users' cooperatives, but they have no link with Panchayats. Appropriate linkage development can tremendously help in improving their status.

Mr. Vas Kalra President; and **Dr. M.L. Dewan** of Rotary Club Delhi (South) Metropolitan mentioned of the Telefood project being developed by them.

Mrs. Kunti Paul, President and Mrs. Lalita Balakrishnan of the All India Women's Conference indicated that sanitation, nutritional inputs and the use of non-conventional energy sources in the rural areas have a significant role to play in development. Explaining their experience they mentioned that ownership of the devices and equipment makes their utilisation much more effective.

The participants appreciated the Project Outline presented by Mr. Ramesh Kumar, and strongly supported the same being considered by UNDP for financial assistance.

WORLD FOOD DAY AWARD - 1998

The World Food Day Awards for the Year 1998 were presented by Dr. N.C. Saxena, Secretary, Ministry of Rural Areas and Employment.

The World Food Day Awards were instituted, jointly by the IAAS and FAO, to recognise contributions of distinguished scientists/experts and mass media personnel to disseminate information and create awareness about issues relating to rural development and agriculture, food and nutrition. Objectivity maintained in the selection of the awardees has raised the stature and acceptability of World Food Day Awards.

The Awards instituted, jointly by the IAAS and FAO, were presented to the following:

(i) *Award for contribution in Print Media –*
Ms. Radhika Singh, Principal Correspondent, *The Economic Times.*

(ii) *Award for TV Programmes –*
TVI

(iii) *Award for Promotion of Food Security of Vulnerable Group–*
All India Women's Conference.

Awards were in the form of a plaque.

APPENDIX-6

THE CONCEPT OF MAHARASHTRA PROJECT MODEL ON FOOD SECURITY AND PANCHAYATI RAJ

RAMESH KUMAR

BACKGROUND FOR PROJECT DESIGN

The Rome Declaration on World Food Security made at the World Food Summit in 1996 reaffirmed[1] "the right of everyone to have access to safe and nutritious food, consistent with the right to adequate food and the fundamental right of everyone to be free from hunger". The Summit while reiterating the basic Human Right to Food, clearly identified the nexus between poverty and food security. It outlined an alternative model based on an integrated approach for achieving food security. The six key elements of the model are given below :

(i) strengthen the capacity of farmers, including indigenous peoples, women and youths, along with local and regional food systems;
(ii) reverse concentration of wealth and power and take action to prevent further concentration;
(iii) change agriculture and food production systems relying on non-renewal resources, which negatively affect the environment, toward a model based on agro-ecological principles;
(iv) proactive policies to eradicate poverty by guaranteeing sustainable livelihoods, employment opportunities for all, improved access of poor to food and resources for agriculture;
(v) deepen participation of peoples' organisations and NGOs; and
(vi) an international code of conduct to guarantee the right to food and ensure food sovereignty ________________.

The Maharashtra Project Model has been designed keeping tenets nos. 1-5 in mind. The Model embraces an integrated development approach to meet the overall objective of developing "an implementation strategy so that food security for the poor is ensured through a self-reliant food production mechanism under the local level village panchayat governance".

The contemporaneous policy contexts in the State, both in the arena of agriculture and rural development have been kept in mind while designing the Project Model. The Agricultural Policy pronounced by the State Government in 1996 emphasises the need to promote environment friendly indigenous agricultural practices. In rural Maharashtra, the three tier Panchayat Raj System is very strongly established in the State. Subsequent to the 73rd Constitutional Amendment, initiatives have been taken to empower the institutions of both the Village Panchayat and Gram Sabha. One-third of the seats in the Panchayat bodies have been reserved for women. Major capacity building efforts are underway in the State of politically educate the new functionaries of the village panchayats about their roles and responsibilities. The current thinking is also to involve village panchayats in managing community level public assets. An enlarged role for the panchayats in the management of the Public Distribution System is also being envisioned.

Further, for designing the Project Model, lessons have been drawn from the IFAD - assisted Maharashtra Rural Credit Project (MRCP) which is being implemented in the State. Some very positive development experiences exist in this area. The MRCP is based on a rural micro credit strategy and women's Self Help Groups. There is great emphasis on the social mobilisation of rural communities. MRCP is being implemented in conjunction with the UNICEF sponsored development philosophy entitled "Convergent Community Action". Our experiences from this experimentation have been distilled for evolving the Project Model. The Model has been conceived within the broad framework of the community level structures which have been put in place under MRCP-CCA.

PROJECT LOCATION

It is proposed to initiate the project as a pilot venture to cover two tribal blocks – Dharni in Amravati District and Mokhada in Thane

District. The justifications for the choice of the Project area are as follows :

(i) A situational analysis to assess the incidence of malnutrition and status of food availability in apposite for drawing the geographical boundaries of the Project. It is an established fact that Maharashtra's tribal pockets are greatly disadvantaged in terms of both these indicators. The tribal areas, especially those in Thane, Amravati and Shule districts report high rates of infant and child mortality and malnutrition. The incidence of seasonal diseases during the monsoons is also very high. These figures are readily available from the MIS for the ICDS Programme. The nexus between child and adult malnutrition is strong. Therefore, the high rates of child mortality and malnutrition are indicative of the low nutritional and health status of these tribal communities.

(ii) The concerns of the State Governments are reflected in a special Scheme called the Navsanjivan Yojana which is being implemented in these areas. It is multifaceted approach to mitigate the causes of health and nutritional deprivations of the tribal population. Besides other measures, the scheme also lays a strong accent on strengthening the PDS in the tribal areas. The UN Project is geared to the same goals and would be complementary in nature by addressing a wider spectrum of issues related to food security, like agricultural production systems, empowerment of the village panchayat, micro level coping strategies to fight food inadequacies, etc.

(iii) The Maharashtra Scheduled Areas Act has given considerable decision making powers to these grassroots institutions in the tribal areas. But their role in the development process is limited to the implementation of programmes like JRY, EAS and others. It is felt that a definite role for the local village panchayats can be carved out for alleviating the imperative concerns related to food insecurity and malnutrition. For this purpose, it is necessary to lay down a precise framework at the village level within which the village panchayats can participate in the exercise, which hitherto has not been precisely done. The Project would provide this opportunity to the panchayats.

(iv) In order to draw upon the lessons flowing out of the MRCP-CCA Programme, it is necessary to locate the project in the districts covered under MRCP-CCA. The Village Development Assembly (VDA), Village Development Council (VDC), and women's SHGs created under MRCP - CCA will provide a ready framework for the Project. Also, an Intersectoral Facilitating Team (IFT) consisting of village level Government functionaries which has been constituted in every village will be available. Both Thane and Amravati districts are covered under MRCP-CCA.

PROJECT GOAL AND OBJECTIVES

The Project Goal can be articulated as: "to empower the tribal village panchayats to take collaborative action for ameliorating the nutritional and food deprivations prevailing in their communities".

The ensuing Project Objectives are multifaceted and can be stated as follows:

(i) to develop individual village panchayat level strategies for augmenting the nutritional and food security status through collaborative community action,

(ii) to empower the village panchayat to develop, implement and monitor a People's Action Plan for Food Security which will include initiatives for employment creation, supply of agricultural inputs like seeds, fertilizers and irrigation and other proactive actions,

(iii) to capacitate the village panchayat to manage community assets and function as a service provider for fair price shops, grain/seed banks,

(iv) to create advocacy for eco-friendly agricultural production systems and awareness about the threat posed by environmental degradation, and

(v) to educate gender groups about desired nutritional and health behaviourial patterns.

SALIENT FEATURES OF PROJECT MODEL

The Process Approach

The underlying approach to augment the food security status adopted under the Project will be a process oriented and empowering one. The process flows are depicted in the Flow Chart. The empowerment of the poor stakeholders is ensured through capacity building and development participation.

Complementarity

The Model is proposed to be implemented in two tribal blocks of the State which are already covered under the Navasanjivan Yojana and the MRCP-CCA Programme. The Project will be complementary in nature to these ongoing initiatives and focus on an integrated set of measures to augment the food and nutritional status of these tribal communities. Since the institution of the village panchayat is not the focal point of the ongoing schemes, there will be no duplication of resources.

Stellar Role of the Village Panchayat

(i) The institution of the village panchayat will play a pivotal role under the Project. Section 49 of the Bombay Village Panchayat provides that a panchayat from among its members may constitute committees for discharging any duties or functions that may be assigned to them by the Panchayat. It is proposed to constitute such a committee to supervise the affairs of the local fair price shop. Administrative orders will be issued in this regard. The actual running of the fair price shops will be left in the hands of the mahila mandal or SHG. It will be responsible for the management of the fair price shops and the seed/ grain banks. The members will be trained to undertake these tasks. It will also earn revenues from the services it renders through these activities.

(ii) The PAP for Food Security will be prepared through the participation of the panchayat, SHG and VDC members.

A major component of this PAP will be the creation of employment opportunities. The Schemes for the creation of employment on public works like EAS and JRY are implemented under the aegis of the village panchayat. Thus, the panchayat will have a significant role in the implementation of the PAP.

(iii) The village panchayat will also retail information about desired agricultural production systems and practices which will be made available free of charge to the BPL families.

(iv) The village panchayat, along with the VDC and SHG members will be involved in monitoring the implementation of the PAP for Food Security.

PROJECT ACTIVITIES

The proposed Project activities can be grouped under eight categories as follows:

A. Baseline Survey

Information gathered through the baseline survey will cover a spectrum of subjects related to food security status, agricultural production systems, nutritional practices, employment opportunities, migration patterns and training requirements. The recent BPL survey information can be taken as a baseline for this research. Information about the profile of the members of the village panchayat and gender groups (SHGs/Mahila Mandal) will be also collected. The degree and quality of development participation of these community organisations will be assessed. The roles played by the VDA, VDC and IFT will be documented.

The survey methodology is of concern here and has to be necessarily participatory in nature. Qualitative research techniques should be used to discern the coping strategies which the poor use for addressing food related inadequacies. Stakeholder participation for the assessment of food insecurity and poverty through the use of PRA techniques like seasonal food calendars and other tools is highly recommended. Especially because such survey results reflect the real concerns of the poor. Also, their involvement at the information gathering stage would promote a feeling of ownership about the Project from the very beginning.

B. Grain Banks and Godowns

Grain and seed banks have been already constituted in the proposed Project areas under the Navsanjivan Yojana. These will be placed under the managerial control of a village panchayat committee. A similar decision will be taken for the running of the fair price shops.

C. Capacity Building

The capacity building initiated under the Project will have to cover different trainees target groups having a variety of learning requirements. These requirements will be identified at the time of the baseline survey. Appropriate trainingware, IEC and extension materials will have to be designed. The training initiated will consists of the following components:

Training of Village Panchayat and SHG Members

Some of the members of Village Panchayat and SHGs will be trained in the use of Participatory Learning and Action (PLA) methods. This expertise will be used by these members to identify in collaboration with community members, problem solving strategies and develop the PAPs for Food Security. These PAPs will be incorporated into the ones being prepared under MRCP-CCA and which focus on overall village development. The IFT members will also facilitate the preparation of the PAPs for Food Security and ensure the necessary flow of information.

The Panchayat and SHGs members will also be trained in the management of fair price shops, grain/seed banks, and village level community assets.

Training of Village Level Service Providers (IFT members)

This will mainly consists of an attitudinal reorientation in existing extension workers. They will be encouraged to initiate problem solving discussions about the adoption of agricultural technologies in order to arrive at environmentally sustainable solutions. They will be required to increasingly focus on collective solutions and actions for the environmental problems which especially beset the small and marginal farmers. Also, the extension workers have to be trained to increase the scale of influence from individual to groups of farmers and transfer besides information, inputs in the form of extension materials. All this will be in the overall context of the PAP for Food Security.

Training of Farmers

Training activities, principally demonstration based, will also be directed at raising the awareness of farmers about eco-friendly agricultural practices, minimising harvest losses, strategies for optimising the use of seeds, fertilisers and irrigation, especially under rain fed conditions.[2]

D. Advocacy for the Production of Nutritious Foods

Advocacy efforts will be made through the extension workers to promote and support an agricultural production strategy which has a focus on coarse grains, pulses and vegetables.[3]

E. Management of Village Level Water Resources

The ongoing rural employment programmes will be utilised to develop village tanks and minor irrigation works which will support and guarantee food production[4]. In Maharashtra, a large number of percolation tanks have been constructed in rural areas. It is proposed to constitute water users' associations to supervise the management of these assets.

F. Community based Monitoring System (Food Security Information System)

The village panchayat and the SHG members will maintain simple formats for monitoring the implementation of the PAP for Food Security. This will include 3-4 community specific indicators and will also serve as an early warning system for any impending nutritional calamity.

G. Advocacy for Desired Health and Nutritional Behaviours

The SHGs established under the MRCP will form the focal points for Nutrition and Health Education. This will be undertaken through extension agents, like the anganwadi worker, ANM and NGO.

H. Advocacy for Eco-friendly Agricultural Production Systems

This will be one of the major activities and will be carried out by the extension agents and NGO. Advocacy will be through a variety of media, such as direct contact with farmer groups, training, distribution of extension materials, dispensation of oral information, etc. The village panchayat will also retail related information.

I. Partnership with NGOs

All the activities detailed above will be executed in partnership with a suitable NGO who has experience in this sector. Especially, the training activities, advocacy for appropriate health, nutritional and agricultural practices will be the responsibility of the NGO.

J. Process Documentation

For sustainability, it is necessary to remember that the process of change is as important as the end results. This process of change is always well documented in stakeholder memory. But for sharing, replication and intergenerational knowledge transfers, documentation through both printed and audio visual media is imperative. This will, therefore, constitute a necessary Project component.

CONCLUSIONS

All the above mentioned project activities are geared to fulfil the stated project goals and objectives. The lines of causation between the activities and a sustained increase in village level food security can be clearly drawn.

The overall project goal is to provide for sustainable food security at the village level. The participation of men, women and community level institutions is essential for arriving at a sustainable solution. This has been provided for in the Project by ensuring exclusive spaces for the participation of all village level actors. These include the Village Panchayat, Women's Groups, water users' associations and farmers.

Further, a sustainable solution is one which will provide for appropriate attitudinal changes in all these actors. This is sought to be addressed by the capacity building of all actors as per their individual learning requirements.

Grain banks and godowns would eliminate the cyclical fluctuations in the supply of foodgrains which is an annual feature. The development of village level tanks and minor irrigation blocks will also result in reducing these cyclical lows in village level food security. By shifting the emphasis of the food production strategy on coarse grains, pulses and vegetables, the local supply of nutritious food will be augmented.

The PAP for Food Security will be designed keeping in mind the requirements of individual village communities. It will be a comprehensive plan of action geared to address issues related to employment creation, supply of agricultural inputs, eco-friendly production systems, efforts for augmenting the supply of nutritious food, and capacity building initiatives for ensuring a change over to desired nutrition and health related behaviours.

It is expected that the project activities will be augmented by efforts at poverty alleviation under IRDP, since poverty is the single most important cause of food insecurity. All these efforts in their totality would largely result in an increase in village level food security.

---

1. See Report of World Food Summit, 13-17 November 1996, FAO, Rome.
2. See point No. III.2(iv) of GOI proposal.
3. See point No. III.2(iii) of GOI proposal.
4. See point No. III.2(v) of GOI proposal.

GLOSSARY OF TERMS

MRPC	Maharashtra Rural Credit Project
CCA	Convergent Community Action
PAP	People's Action Plan
SHG	Self Help Group
VDC	Village Development Council
VDA	Village Development Assembly
IFT	Intersectoral Facilitating Team
PDS	Public Distribution System
EAS	Employment Assurance Scheme
JRY	Jawahar Rozgar Yojana
ICDS	Integrated Child Development Services
BPL	Below Poverty Line
PLA	Participatory Learning and Action
ANM	Auxiliary Nurse Midwife
NGO	Non-Governmental Organisation
IRDP	Integrated Rural Development Programme

INDEX